GW00786585

CON

What is Booktrust?

Booktrust is the charity committed to bringing books and people together. The Children's Literature Team at Booktrust is concerned with all aspects of the children's book world and, as an independent organisation, is uniquely placed to provide entirely impartial advice to everybody interested in children's reading. We run projects (such as **Bookstart** and **National Children's Book Week**), administer book prizes (**Sainsbury's Baby Book Award**, the **Nestlé Smarties Book Prize** and the **Booktrust Teenage Prize**), produce a quarterly magazine, *Booktrusted News* and host a number of websites, including our dedicated children's site, **www.booktrusted.com**.

What is the Best Book Guide?

The Best Book Guide for Children and Young Adults is the new name for *100 Best Books*, the annual pick of the best paperback fiction from the previous calendar year. With so many excellent books published for children, we found it increasingly difficult to select just 100 titles each year. Therefore, we have expanded this year's publication to include even more titles for a range of ages, from babies to teenagers. The books we have included are intended to represent a wide variety of writing styles and subjects. They should provide a starting point, introducing new authors and genres and re-acquainting you with familiar ones. There are funny stories, animal tales, historical fiction, thrillers, books dealing with social issues and topics appropriate for discussion, as well as some of the more unusual and original books of the year.

Who is the Guide for?

Parents, teachers, librarians, children – in fact anyone interested in the world of children's books.

How does the Guide work?

The guide is organised into colour coded age categories, ranging from baby books to teenage fiction. Within each section, the books are arranged in approximate age order. In addition, there is a Reading Age (**RA**), indicating the suggested age necessary to read the text and an Interest Level (**IL**) which indicates the full age-range for which it is likely to appeal most. The age categories are meant only as a broad guideline and the boundaries should be seen as flexible. Many books listed here will appeal to a wide age-range, including adults! Each entry has a colour picture of the book jacket, bibliographic details for easy ordering at bookshops and libraries, and a short review. All books listed are paperback, unless otherwise stated. At the end of the guide there is a title and author index, as well as a subject index, listing some of the major themes running through the books.

How do we choose the books?

Booktrust receives a copy of nearly every book published for children in the UK. We have an extensive team of expert reviewers, ranging from Booktrust staff to teachers, librarians, writers, parents and people from the book world. This diversity of experience and viewpoints ensures there is something for every taste, interest and ability. We invite submissions from publishers and select some of the outstanding books that have caught our eye throughout 2002. Of course there are many more excellent books that we didn't have room for, but the Guide should be seen as an introduction to quality fiction rather than a definitive list.

What's new?

The Best Book Guide concentrates on new paperback fiction, but there are many other types of books to enjoy. See our small selection of Poetry Books and Non-fiction titles on pages 68 and 69.

Sarah Harrington
Editor

First Books for Babies

Books for babies should be bold, bright and colourful – and able to withstand lots of rough treatment and occasional orange juice spills! It's never too early to introduce your baby to books. All the different formats available (bath books, cloth books, board books) encourage young children to become familiar with the concept of holding a book and turning the pages. The best books for this age group encourage a child to participate actively by touching, pointing and identifying familiar objects, and enjoying simple stories and rhymes.

Illustration taken from *Head, Shoulders, Knees and Toes...* by Annie Kubler, reproduced by permission of Child's Play (International) Ltd

Ring Ring!
Caroline Davis

Little Orchard (Board Book) ISBN: 1 84121 432 9 £2.99

Illustrated with shimmery foil to provide lots of visual excitement, this sturdy little board book in the *Shimmery Dinkies* series is packed with colourful, familiar objects. The reader is encouraged to say aloud the related sounds of each object, such as the 'tick tock' of the clock, and 'splish splash' in the bath. The chunky pages will stand plenty of wear and tear, ensuring that this will become a firm favourite with the very young.

One Bear, One Dog
Paul Stickland

Ragged Bears (Board Book) ISBN: 1 85714 255 1 £6.99

Fun, lively illustrations fill every page of this board book for young children. 'One bear' is joined by 'one dog' and so on, until by the end of the book, an assortment of animals is dancing and skipping in a line across the page. A baby will enjoy sharing this with an adult, and will love the surprise guest at the end! A delightful first book, providing a very early introduction to numbers, counting and animals.

Head, Shoulders, Knees and Toes...
illustrated by Annie Kubler

Child's Play (International) Ltd (Board Book)
ISBN: 0 85953 728 5 £3.99

This is a happy book for babies and toddlers, a book that no one will be able to listen to and remain sitting still! The text invites the reader to sing the familiar action rhyme, and the joyous pictures of babies demand that everyone joins in. The babies take over the book and are colourful, active and enticing – and set against a white background, they're great for the youngest of children to focus on.

Snail
Fiona Watt, illustrated by Rachel Wells
Usborne (Cloth Book) ISBN: 0 7460 5185 9 £4.99

Stan the snail follows a trail of discovery through the garden to find his friend Sam. This beautiful cloth book is bursting with bright colours, textures, and even sounds, and there is plenty to discuss as Sam goes on his way. This is a very appealing and exciting 'touchy-feely' book, which would make a lovely present.

The Bear Went Over the Mountain
John Prater
Red Fox ISBN: 0 09 943917 4 £3.99

Baby Bear and Grandbear make a welcome return in this appealing picture book for the very young. The popular rhyme is brought to life with lively pictures of the two bears playing in a mountain of bedclothes. Babies will enjoy singing along and the gentle accompanying pictures make learning the rhyme fun.

Let's Have Fun
Verna Wilkins, illustrated by Pamela Venus
Tamarind (Board Book) ISBN: 1 870516 54 0 £3.99

This little board book, showing a child enjoying playing at the park, is full of movement, and has appealing colour pictures, with an accompanying simple, rhyming text. This is a good book for sharing, as babies and toddlers will recognise and delight in the familiar everyday activities.

Night, Night, Baby
Marie Birkinshaw, illustrated by Kate Merritt
Ladybird Books (Board Book) ISBN: 0 7214 8135 3 £4.99

Night, Night, Baby sparkles from the cover to the final page. It's a slightly larger than usual board book, with bright, bold colours, big flaps to lift, and a rhyming text that children will love to hear again and again. The babies hidden behind the flaps fill the pages, so are good for very young children to focus on, and bound to raise a chuckle. A lovely book for bedtime, as it has a warm, very satisfying ending.

What Shall We Do With The Boo Hoo Baby?
Cressida Cowell, illustrated by Ingrid Godon
Campbell Books (Board Book) ISBN: 0 333 98477 3 £4.99

The Boo-Hoo Baby won't stop crying, so the animals who are looking after him try all the usual solutions, such as feeding him, bathing him and playing with him, but nothing seems to work. There are lots of farmyard noises to join in with and amusing, expressive pictures. This is a lovely book to share and will appeal to babies and adults alike.

Fab Baby! Dressing
Elaine Field
Little Tiger Press (Board Book) ISBN: 1 85430 829 7 £3.99

Each page of this unusual board book shows another stage of a baby dressing. The young reader is encouraged to turn the wheel to reveal pictures of various items of clothing and match them to the simple text. The colourful illustrations are full of humour and children will enjoy searching for Jake's shoes or Laura's dress. As well as providing entertainment, this interactive book will encourage children to recognise a variety of familiar objects, as well as improving their motor skills and co-ordination. Look out for other titles in the series (Colours, Numbers, Eating).

Picture Story Books 2-6

These books are ideal for sharing with pre-school children and are full of bright and attractive illustrations. They should encourage plenty of discussion and allow children to start learning words and to play an active role in the storytelling. Children will definitely have their favourite stories and pictures and will ask for them over and over again. Once they begin to learn to read themselves, they will often return to these early favourites.

Illustration by Chris Riddell, taken from *Rabbit's Wish* by Paul Stewart and Chris Riddell, reproduced by permission of Andersen Press

Daddy's Lullaby

Tony Bradman, illustrated by Jason Cockcroft
Bloomsbury ISBN: 0 7475 5559 1 £4.99

When Daddy gets home late on a Friday night after a hard week at work, everyone in the house is asleep – except for the baby. Dad and baby take a walk through the darkened house, visiting the rest of the sleeping family before settling down to a lullaby and a nap downstairs. This is a familiar story, beautifully and simply told, with a lullaby (Rock-a-Bye Baby) at the end. The illustrations are positively stunning and give a really intimate feel. Dads and their babies will love this. **RA 5+/IL 2-4**

Flora's Blanket

Debi Gliori
Little Orchard (Board Book) ISBN: 1·84121 064 1 £3.99

Flora the rabbit can't get off to sleep because her blanket is lost and nothing else will do to take its place. The illustrations are a delight, and all the family members offer suggestions in ways that perfectly reflect a human family. This is a warm book for the end of the day, with positive images of reading, as one little rabbit brother always has his nose in a book. The story is one you simply won't mind reading over and over again. This little board book version includes some 'touch-and-feel' pages too.
RA 5+/IL 2-5

Louie Loves His Little Sister

Yves Got, English text by Simona Sideri
Zero to Ten ISBN: 1 84089 248 X £4.99

Louie and his little sister are a toddler and baby rabbit respectively. The very simple text describes all the things Louie and his little sister like to do together, things that every toddler would recognise as part of having a new baby around the house. It also acknowledges that, sometimes, little sisters can be no fun at all! With distinctive, colourful illustrations, this is a good book to help deal with the arrival of a sibling in the household.
RA 5+/IL 2-5

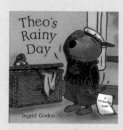

Theo's Rainy Day
Ingrid Godon
Campbell Books (Board Book) ISBN: 0 333 96603 1 £4.99
It is raining outside so Theo and Alice cannot go out to play. Then Theo has a great idea – they can play dressing-up and pretend to be sailors. They find some suitable clothes, turn an old trunk into their boat and are all ready to sail on the high seas, face pirates and have dangerous adventures. Their playful imaginations allow the children to enjoy their game and discover a delicious treasure at the end of their voyage. This is an amusing board book with lift-the-flap pages. The stunning illustrations are highly appealing and full of colourful surprises.
RA 5+/IL 2-5

I Want a Sister
Tony Ross
Andersen Press (Board Book) ISBN: 1 84270 103 7 £4.99
This is one of a series of books about the loveable, yet demanding, Little Princess, and is packed with fun and gentle learning. The Little Princess is pleased to hear about the new baby – but only if it's a sister. The usual characters – the Queen, the King, the Doctor, the Maid, the Admiral and the Prime Minister – try to prepare her for the other possibility, but have no success. Of course, the Little Princess comes round in the end, and manages to smile at the Little Prince. Tony Ross is a genius; his characters are wonderfully expressed and the early learning he offers is always completely painless. **RA 5+/IL 2-5**

Platypus
Chris Riddell
Puffin ISBN: 0 14 056777 1 £4.99
This is the story of Platypus, an endearing character who loves collecting things. After one particularly successful day at the beach, Platypus returns triumphantly with a beautiful curly shell to add to his collection. However, when he wakes the next day he is baffled to discover that his shell has gone. The simple, bold illustrations are satisfying and full of character. This is a beautiful and heart-warming book with a gentle message about respecting the natural world. **RA 6+/IL 2-6**

Little Robots
Mike Brownlow
Ragged Bears ISBN: 1 85714 257 8 £4.99
Little robots come in all shapes and sizes, from bright, shiny and tiny, to trendy, spotty and scruffy. In this amusing picture book, children are introduced to the most colourful characters, each decorated with cheerful patterns and crazy gadgets. The rhythmical text and bright illustrations make this a highly original and inventive picture book and the range of adjectives provides much opportunity for comparisons. **RA 5+/IL 3-6**

Oscar and Arabella
Neal Layton
Hodder Children's Books ISBN: 0 340 79720 7 £4.99
Oscar and Arabella are two loveable woolly mammoths who spend their days exploring, skating and trying to avoid wild and dangerous animals – humans! This original and amusing picture book introduces young children to unusual characters in familiar situations. The lively illustrations enhance the simple text, making this an enjoyable book to share. **RA 5+/IL 3-6**

Meg up the Creek
Helen Nicoll, illustrated by Jan Pieńkowski
Puffin ISBN: 0 14 056893 X £4.99
Meg the witch, Mog her cat, and Owl, travel up the creek in their canoe. They are all very hungry, so stop off in a wood to search for food, but seem unable to find anything to cook for their supper. Luckily, Meg has brought along emergency supplies in her cauldron, but just as they are about to cook the contents, an unexpected visitor changes the course of events and Meg has to make a spell to save the day. It is great to see these classic characters making a comeback. The story has lots of action and humour to entertain the reader and the bright, colourful illustrations are a delight. **RA 5+/IL 3-6**

Why Am I So Small?
Eun Ju Kim
Siphano Picture Books ISBN: 1 903078 62 8 £4.99
Ollie is a young mouse who can't understand why he hasn't grown as big as Mark, his elder brother. Mark explains that in order to grow fast he will need to exercise, eat plenty of healthy food and get lots of sleep. Ollie follows his advice to the letter, but when he goes to the playground the following day, he realises that things have not worked out as originally planned. In the end Ollie learns a very important lesson: that to become big you have to start small. This is an amusing picture book, which also tackles a concern that many young children have. A perfect story for sharing and reading aloud, with warm watercolour illustrations. **RA 6+/IL 2-6**

There's a House Inside My Mummy
Giles Andreae, illustrated by Vanessa Cabban
Orchard Books ISBN: 1 84121 068 4 £4.99
This is just the book to explain to inquisitive children what's going on inside mum during pregnancy. Through the rhyming text, a toddler explains why his mum's tummy is getting so big, and what he expects to happen. Soft, colourful pictures, full of domestic detail, contribute to the book's humorous approach, but also allow for discussion in greater depth, if desired.
RA 6+/IL 2-7

Follow the Line
Simone Lia
Egmont ISBN: 0 7497 4858 3 £4.99
Bruce's mum is baking a cake, but his trip to the moon can't wait and so he sets off, following 'a very long line' on the floor. He is directed on his way by all sorts of strange creatures, until at last he reaches the moon (or is it the living room?) and they have a party. Suddenly, he remembers the cake and arrives back 'just in time'. Child-like illustrations, strong primary colours and, of course, the line which Bruce follows, all combine to give this book plenty of toddler appeal. A quietly quirky celebration of the power of make-believe. **RA 5+/IL 3-7**

No More Kissing!
Emma Chichester Clark
Collins ISBN: 0 00 713105 4 £4.99

Kissing drives Momo the monkey crazy, but unfortunately for him, his friends and family kiss one another at every opportunity. When his little brother is born, everyone kisses him too, but this doesn't stop his incessant crying. Momo explains that obviously his little brother hates kissing too, and he tries to find other ways to stop him crying. He manages to placate the baby, and then, unable to resist his brother's sweet smile, surprises himself by kissing him! This book has adorable characters and a lovely, unpredictable ending. **RA 5+/IL 3-7**

The Three Little Pigs
Nick Sharratt and Stephen Tucker
Macmillan ISBN: 0 333 96397 0 £4.99

This retelling in rhyme of the traditional fairy tale is very funny, and yet sticks accurately to the story of the Three Little Pigs. It is superbly illustrated and uses flaps very cleverly, so that the reader can help the pigs build their houses and then demolish them when the wolf starts huffing and puffing. The rhyming text also makes it suitable as an introduction to reading for the very young. The best 'flaps' book to be published for a long time, which neither children nor adults will tire of. (Not suitable for children under 36 months.) **RA 7+/IL 3-7**

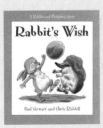

Rabbit's Wish
Paul Stewart, illustrated by Chris Riddell
Andersen Press ISBN: 1 84270 089 8 £4.99

Rabbit and Hedgehog are best friends, but as Hedgehog is a night creature and Rabbit a day creature, they are never able to spend much time with each other. Rabbit wishes they could be together for a whole day, and when it rains heavily one day, his wish comes true. Both their homes are flooded and Hedgehog swims across the lake to check that his friend is safe. They are delighted to be unexpectedly together and spend the day playing and having fun. This is a wonderful book, which explores the nature of kindness and friendship. The relationship between Rabbit and Hedgehog is touching and the illustrations are absolutely stunning, bringing the text to life. **RA 7+/IL 3-7**

Old Bear's All-Together Painting
Jane Hissey
Red Fox ISBN: 0 09 941313 2 £4.99
Old Bear is about to frame his small painting of Little Bear. The other toys want to paint their own pictures too, but the problem is that only one picture frame remains, and it is a big one. Old Bear's solution is that they each produce a painting and he will combine them to produce one big picture. With one or two colourful accidents along the way, the project is finally finished to everyone's satisfaction. This story could be a useful back-up for a class art activity and young children will be enchanted by the detailed, highly atmospheric illustrations. **RA 7+/IL 3-7**

Tatty Ratty
Helen Copper
Picture Corgi ISBN: 0 552 54630 5 £5.99
Molly is very upset when she loses her beloved soft toy, Tatty Ratty. Her parents console her by helping her to imagine all the wonderful adventures Tatty Ratty is having while he is away. They are sure he must have met lots of interesting characters, such as the Three Bears, Cinderella, pirates, dragons and even the Man in the Moon. This atmospheric book will comfort children who have lost a favourite toy and will take the reader on a magical journey through a land of dreams and fantasy. **RA 7+/IL 3-7**

Claude and the Big Surprise
David Wojtowycz
Gullane Children's Books ISBN: 1 86233 384 X £4.99
Claude, the young polar bear, spends a week with Great Aunt Annie in the Arctic, where he skis, builds a snowbear and has lots of fun in the snow. He has a great time, but he misses Mum and Dad, so is pleased when it is time to go home, especially when he sees the big surprise waiting for him – a brand new sister! This simple story has bright, colourful illustrations, and is ideal for young children who are expecting a new brother or sister. **RA 7+/IL 3-7**

Don't Cry, Sly!
Henriette Barkow, illustrated by Richard Johnson, Chinese translation by Sylvia Denham
Mantra ISBN: 1 85269 651 6 £7.50

Sly's mum is always bossing him around and the poor little fox is fed up with the way he is treated. Next door lives Little Red Hen, who becomes very nervous when Sly is sent to find a roast chicken for dinner. However, the quick-thinking hen comes up with a plan to suit them all. The pictures are wonderful, expressive, and highly atmospheric. This dual language picture book is written in Chinese and English, and is available in 20 other language editions. A wonderful book to read aloud, it is ideal for children with English as a second language and would lend itself well to classroom use, particularly in multicultural schools. **RA 6+/IL 3-7**

The Big Bad Rumour
Jonathan Meres, illustrated by Jacqueline East
Red Fox ISBN: 0 09 940059 6 £4.99

When Goose learns that a big bad hopping-mad wolf is on his way, he quickly runs to warn the other animals. In their panic, they mishear what he says and absurd rumours quickly circulate of a shopping-mad wolf in a wig! The dramatic tension increases throughout the amusing tale and the clever twist at the end will make young readers laugh out loud. Colourful and expressive illustrations will capture young imaginations, while the hilarious, repetitive text makes it ideal for reading aloud.
RA 6+/IL 3-7

The Dance of the Dinosaurs
Colin and Jacqui Hawkins
Collins ISBN: 0 00 711444 3 £4.99

Georgie and Dee are frightened by a noisy thunderstorm one night, so Cat takes them on a journey in a hot air balloon to show them where the storm is coming from. They arrive in a land of dinosaurs and discover that the loud crashes and bangs in the sky are caused by the stomping Dance of the Dinosaurs! The children eagerly join in the fun, and at the end of the dance, return home exhausted to a peaceful night's sleep. This colourful picture book for the under-fives will make an ideal story for reading aloud before bedtime. The illustrations follow the rhyming text beautifully and have great 'child appeal'.
RA 6+/IL 3-7

Rattletrap Car
Phyllis Root, illustrated by Jill Barton
Walker Books ISBN: 0 7445 8932 0 £4.99
It's a hot, hot day, and the children are clamouring for a trip to the lake. Dad is doubtful that their rattletrap car will make it, but they set out armed with cookies, drinks and toys. Bit by bit the car disintegrates, but the family ingeniously get it on the move again and eventually reach their destination. With off-beat rhymes and repeated wacky words, perfect for joining in, this is a delightful read, with scrumptious warm illustrations. Deserves to be loved until the covers fall off. **RA 6+/IL 3-7**

Splosh!
Philippe Corentin, translated from French by Sarah Pakenham
Andersen Press ISBN: 0 86264 589 1 £3.99
A very hungry wolf spies what he thinks is a round cheese at the bottom of a well, but when he climbs down, he realises that it is just the reflection of the moon. Finding himself trapped in the well, he tricks a passing pig to rescue him. Satisfyingly, the sly, greedy wolf gets what he deserves in the end. This is a humorous, carefully designed book, and the long, slender format adds an extra dimension to the colourful illustrations. **RA 6+/IL 3-7**

My Cat's Weird
Lydia Monks
Egmont ISBN: 1 4052 0166 5 £4.99
Wonderfully funny, colourful illustrations show readers just how weird this cat is. He's positively human: he reads books, eats with a knife and fork, and rides a bike. It's all very embarrassing for his small owner, until one day the cat makes an aeroplane and whisks him off for tea and cakes in the jungle. The typeface mirrors the action, swirling and swooping and changing size. An excellent book to encourage readers to create their own fantasies. **RA 6+/IL 3-7**

Quack, Quack!
Philippe Dupasquier
Andersen Press ISBN: 1 84270 112 6 £4.99
Vicki's new neighbour, Mrs Spikes, appears to be a charming old lady, and the whole family thinks that her pet duck is really exciting. However, when the duck interrupts everything they want to do by quacking non-stop, the family begins to think very differently about her. As their relationship becomes increasingly fraught, Vicki's dad comes up with an idea to force Mrs Spikes to get rid of her duck, but his plan has an unexpected – and very positive – outcome. Adorned with delightfully animated illustrations, this book encourages thoughtful discussion about consideration for others. **RA 6+/IL 4-7**

Five Little Fiends
Sarah Dyer
Bloomsbury ISBN: 0 7475 5949 X £4.99
Five little fiends live inside five statues and every day they come out to admire the world around them. Then, one day, they each decide to take their favourite bit of the world and keep it for themselves. They take the sky, land, moon, sun and sea and hide them inside their statues, only to discover that the treasures are only really beautiful when put together and shared with others. An original approach to teaching about sharing, with beautifully simple and striking illustrations. **RA 5+/IL 4-7**

Good News! Bad News!
Colin McNaughton
Collins ISBN: 0 00 664772 3 £4.99
This is a delightfully funny book, which will amuse children and adults alike. It has a simple but effective style, with a short 'good news' statement followed by a linking 'bad news' statement. The central figure is a young boy who is depicted with some brilliant facial expressions, showing exactly how he feels as he receives the good and bad news. The illustrations are great fun and they illuminate the text effectively. The good news/bad news format could lead to some good oral, written, or drama activities in the classroom. **RA 5+/IL 4-7**

Beginning to Read 5-8

The books in this section are ideal for children who are just starting to read for themselves, or they can be read aloud to help build confidence. They have been selected to complement the books and schemes they will be encountering at school. It is important to continue the habit of reading together at home so that children recognise reading as a worthwhile and enjoyable leisure activity. Bright and lively illustrations are still important to capture the child's imagination.

Illustration taken from *What's Cooking, Jamela?* by Niki Daly, reproduced by permission of Frances Lincoln

The Adventures of Bert
Allan Ahlberg, illustrated by Raymond Briggs
Puffin ISBN: 0 14 056754 2 £4.99

In Bert – a big, accident-prone, innocent abroad – these two popular children's authors have created a classic comic character. Only Bert could start by putting on a shirt and end up miles away on the back of a lorry. His misadventures lead to lots of slapstick fun and the straightforward text encourages plenty of reader interaction, as we're invited to 'say hello' to Bert and his long-suffering wife, Mrs Bert, but warned to 'turn the page quietly' in case we wake the baby. A deceptively simple picture book with great appeal for adults and children. Perfect for sharing. **RA 5+/IL 4-7**

Room on the Broom
Julia Donaldson, illustrated by Axel Scheffler
Macmillan ISBN: 0 333 90338 2 £5.99

As a witch flies with her cat on her broomstick, the wind blows her hat from her head. Luckily, a friendly dog rescues it and, as a reward, is invited to travel with them on the broom. Throughout the tale, they encounter a series of other characters, each of whom helps the witch to recover various possessions that she loses along the way. The rhythmical text makes it ideal for reading aloud and the superb, vibrant illustrations create convincing and expressive characters. This hilarious story, from the award-winning team that created *The Gruffalo,* is sure to be a big hit with young children. **RA 6+/IL 3-7**

Maybe One Day
Frances Thomas, illustrated by Ross Collins
Bloomsbury ISBN: 0 7475 5569 9 £4.99

Little Monster investigates the exciting explorations he would 'maybe' like to make when he's just a little bit older and ready to leave his parents. With each suggestion, Father Monster voices some of Little Monster's own fears, but Little Monster gives rational responses to each, thereby enabling him (and the readers) to face and resolve these fears about growing up. The brightly coloured pictures, while definitely extra-terrestrial, are filled with reassuring domestic detail, and the text design and placing mirrors the meaning. **RA 6+/IL 4-8**

The Yo-Yo King
Vic Parker, illustrated by David Whittle
Oxford University Press ISBN: 0 19 272487 8 £4.99
A story in rhyme, about friendship and the yo-yo craze.
Energetic, quirkily drawn, multi-ethnic street scenes accompany
the verse on each bright, colour-filled page, as readers learn of
the individual skills of the children. They are joined by talented
newcomer Kareem Hakeem, but remain uncertain about him
until he reveals his amazing yo-yo control. By the end of the
story, however, he is valued even more as a friend than as a yo-
yo wizard. **RA 6+/IL 5-8**

Steve's Sunday Blues
Neal Layton
Hodder Children's Books ISBN: 0 340 79722 3 £4.99
It is Sunday evening and Steve is fed up. He has that horrible
feeling everyone gets when it is the end of the weekend and
Monday is rapidly approaching. Dad suggests going out for a
walk, while Mum proposes visiting Auntie Vera. When the big
moment finally arrives, Steve finds out that going to school is
not so bad after all. This original and inventive picture book, with
distinctive, lively illustrations, will entertain readers and help to
overcome those Sunday blues. **RA 6+/IL 4-8**

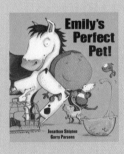

Emily's Perfect Pet
Jonathan Shipton, illustrated by Garry Parsons
Gullane Children's Books ISBN: 1 86233 421 8 £4.99
Emily wants a pet for her birthday, but her parents protest that
everything she suggests is unsuitable for one reason or another.
By the time she gets to her final choice, she's given up hope –
but as she stomps out into the garden, she gets a wonderful
surprise! Imaginative, vibrant pictures illustrate what might have
happened if Emily had been given the pets on her list, and show
why the present she receives is the best one after all. This
entertaining book provides an unusual way to provoke
discussion about what pets to choose and how to look after
them. **RA 6+/IL 5-8**

I Am Not Sleepy and I Will Not Go To Bed
Lauren Child
Orchard Books ISBN: 1 84121 078 1 £4.99
Charlie's little sister, Lola, clearly loves delaying bedtime and he has to use his powers of logic and diplomacy to persuade her to go to bed. The illustrations and comments from the little girl reflect the way in which a child mixes the imaginary and real worlds. The layout of the text is very varied, combining images of relevant objects with the story. There are a number of pages that deal with such topics as time and actions, which could prompt discussion or follow-up activities. This humorous look at bedtime will strike a chord with many children and adults.
RA 6+/IL 5-8

The Brave Little Grork
Kathryn Cave, illustrated by Nick Maland
Hodder Children's Books ISBN: 0 340 74678 5 £4.99
Grorks are shy, easily-frightened creatures, and the one in this story is no exception. When his friend, the greep, suggests going for a walk to the wood, the grork is terrified of all sorts of things, particularly of running into the scary turple. Throughout the journey, the grork leaps into bushes and ditches to escape a variety of horrors, which in fact always turn out to be the kindly flurg. This delightful tale, with attractive illustrations, shows how brave the little grork is: despite all his anxieties, he continues on his journey to the wood, and so confronts his many fears.
RA 6+/IL 4-8

Whatever Wanda Wanted
Jude Wisdom
Gullane Children's Books ISBN: 1 86233 300 9 £4.99
Wanda is a spoilt little girl who always gets her own way. When she sets her sights on a big kite that is not even for sale, she gets what she wants as usual. However, the kite teaches her a lesson, transporting her to a tiny desert island where she has to learn to survive. The use of collage, ink and paints is highly effective and brings this amusing cautionary tale to life.
RA 6+/IL 4-8

The Scarecrow's Hat
Ken Brown
Andersen Press ISBN: 1 84270 101 0 £4.99
Scarecrow has a very nice hat, but would prefer a walking stick to lean his tired arms on. Badger has a walking stick to prop open his door, but would rather tie it open with a ribbon. As she tours the farm, Chicken finds that lots of creatures have something they would like to swap for something else – and if she's clever, she can make everyone happy and get a good deal for herself into the bargain. This lovely tale, with beautiful, full-page, watercolour illustrations, has a really traditional feel.
RA 7+/IL 3-7

The Witch's Children
Ursula Jones, illustrated by Russell Ayto
Orchard Books ISBN: 1 84121 114 1 £4.99
On a trip to the park, the witch's children meet Gemma, who is sailing her toy boat. When the wind blows it over in the middle of the pond, the children use their magic powers to help, but instead they make the situation even worse. Luckily, their mum arrives just in time to sort everything out! This book has been wonderfully designed, and the text is in perfect harmony with the incredibly funny illustrations. Each character is full of expression and humour, making this a very enjoyable picture book to share. **RA 6+/IL 3-8**

The Hoppameleon
Paul Geraghty
Red Fox ISBN: 0 09 940853 8 £4.99
This story follows the quest of a frog who endeavours to find two things: his identity and a friend. Various creatures recognise aspects of themselves in him and they try to help him work out who he is. The illustrations are bright and bold, highlighting some of the key characteristics of a frog. There is some beautiful use of language, including similes, alliteration and onomatopoeia. **RA 6+/IL 3-7**

What's Cooking, Jamela?
Niki Daly
Frances Lincoln ISBN: 0 7112 1705 X £5.99
This is the second story about Jamela, a little girl who lives in a
South African township. Everyone is looking forward to
Christmas and Mama buys a chicken to fatten up for the special
meal. But Jamela calls the chicken Christmas, feeds her and
grows fonder of her as she gets fatter. Finally, she saves
Christmas from the pot by declaring that, 'Christmas is a friend
and you can't eat friends!' So Mama makes stuffed marrow
instead and everyone is happy, including Christmas. This is a
warm and funny family story, with vibrant illustrations full of
domestic detail, both familiar and exotic. **RA 6+/IL 4-8**

Cold Jac
Rob Lewis
Pont Books ISBN: 1 84323 117 4 £4.95
Jac works on a farm on a cold, rainy hillside in Wales and finds
it hard to keep warm. His Nain (Granny) offers to make him a
sweater but her knitting skills are rather rusty and she manages
to produce a string of garments which are too small, too big,
have too many armholes and so on. Jac, however, puts all her
creations to good use, and soon he, and all his animals, are as
warm as toast. The illustrations beautifully depict a wild and
windswept Welsh farm and Nain's many gifts of colourful
knitwear. A funny and interactive, rhyming story, sure to become
a favourite with both parents and children. **RA 7+/IL 3-7**

Little Blue and the Terrible Jokes
Margaret Ryan, illustrated by Andy Ellis
Hodder Children's Books ISBN: 0 340 85211 9 £4.99
Little Blue is a cute little penguin, who is visited by his cousin
Penni. She is an extremely annoying character who insists that
her jokes and tricks (not always very kind) are hilariously funny.
Needless to say, she has to be taught a lesson she won't forget.
The balance of text and pictures makes this an ideal book for
early readers, and there is a good deal of repetition to help
young learners. They may even find some of the jokes funny!
RA 6+/IL 4-8

The Sandcastle
M.P. Robertson
Frances Lincoln ISBN: 0 7112 1807 2 £5.99
Reality and fantasy combine to produce an enchanting story that takes the reader into the past to experience a magical adventure. Jack builds a sandcastle and finds a shell with magical powers. He wishes his sandcastle was as big as a real one and that he was King. However, when his wishes come true, he realises that being King is not that much fun after all and is relieved to return to his old self. This clever book has an engaging plot and amazing illustrations. Ideal for a child who is just beginning to read. **RA 6+/IL 4-8**

Winnie's Magic Wand
Korky Paul
Oxford University Press ISBN: 0 19 272541 6 £4.99
Wacky witch Winnie washes her party dress to impress her audience of witches at the Magic Show. Unfortunately, her wand is also washed by mistake and she finds out, much to her horror, that her spells no longer work as they should. Her trusty black cat, Wilbur, saves the day by buying a new wand, a trick one, which wows the audience at the show. The illustrations are wonderful, with many humorous touches and excellent detail which children will love exploring. **RA 6+/IL 5-8**

Beware of Girls
Tony Blundell
Puffin ISBN: 0 140 56660 0 £4.99
Wolf is hungry; looking at the pictures in his favourite fairy tale has made him hungrier still. He sets out to capture the little girl in the nearby cottage, but the wolf is far from cunning and the little girl neatly turns the tables on him every time. Soon she has him running around and fetching all her favourite foods. We almost feel sorry for the wolf as he is dispatched into the wide blue yonder – still with an empty tummy. A brilliant combination of very funny text and lively, comic illustrations, this is Little Red Riding Hood with a thoroughly modern twist. **RA 6+/IL 5-8**

The Race
Caroline Repchuk, illustrated by Alison Jay
Templar Publishing ISBN: 1 84011 104 6 £4.99
Hare and Tortoise are both going to New York and they decide
to make a race of the journey. Hare rushes off in his usual
manner and is soon in trouble, but slow and steady Tortoise has
a cunning plan. The story follows their roundabout journey right
up to the finishing line, where Hare makes a grand entrance,
but did he beat Tortoise? A lyrical retelling of Aesop's fable and
Verne's *Around the World in Eighty Days*, beautifully
complemented by the vibrant illustrations. A great book.
RA 6+/IL 4-8

Spinderella
Julia Donaldson, illustrated by Liz Pichon
Egmont (Blue Go Bananas) ISBN: 1 4052 0072 3 £3.99
Spinderella is desperate to learn how to count, but her spider
family just don't want to know. That is, until her Hairy Godmother
helps her and, at last, she and her many siblings can play
football, organise the teams and count the goals – all thanks to
numbers! An engaging story with facts and activities about
football, counting and halving. **RA 6+/IL 5-8**

Wizzil
William Steig, illustrated by Quentin Blake
Bloomsbury ISBN: 0 7475 5098 0 £4.99
Wizzil the witch is thoroughly bored, so she turns into a fly and
sets off to make mischief at Frimp Farm. Old Dewitt Frimp
detests flies, so Wizzil becomes a workglove, making him swat
everything in sight – except flies. Finally, he flings the glove into
the river and then dives in to save Wizzil from drowning. But
instead of a witch, he finds himself rescuing a sweet, old lady.
The river has washed her nastiness clean away. Of course, they
fall in love and Wizzil is never bored again. A highly original tale
of the redemptive power of love (and a good bath),
complemented by Quentin Blake's superbly funny illustrations.
RA 7+/IL 5-8

The Tin Forest
Helen Ward, illustrated by Wayne Anderson
Templar Publishing ISBN: 1 84011 108 9 £4.99
An old man lives alone in the middle of nowhere, surrounded by everybody else's rubbish. He dreams about living in a beautiful place and realises that he can make life better. He uses all of the rubbish to create his own forest, complete with tin flowers and animals. A real bird comes to the forest, and soon the old man's world is transformed into a place of beauty. A simple story that comes to life and is made special by the stunning illustrations. **RA 6+/IL 6-8**

A Tale of Two Wolves
Susan Kelly, illustrated by Lizzie Finlay
Red Fox (Flying Foxes) ISBN: 0 09 943213 7 £3.99
The two wolves of the title are identical in every respect, except that one is good and has two brown eyes, and one is bad and has one brown and one blue eye. It's a tiny difference that lands the good wolf in court, when he's accused of all the fairy-tale crimes that the bad wolf is responsible for. This very simple story introduces sophisticated notions of guilt, proof and decision-making processes to very young readers. Told with great humour, it is complemented by colourful, animated illustrations and has ideas for related activities at the end of the book.
RA 6+/IL 6-8

Captain Pepper's Pets
Sally Grindley, illustrated by David Parkins
Kingfisher (I Am Reading) ISBN: 0 7534 0576 8 £3.99
Captain Pepper is a bully. He terrorises his inept crew into seeking out a new and sensational pet, so that he will become the envy and admiration of the pirate world. His hapless sailors round up and then manage to lose a variety of animals, much to the anger of their captain. In deep trouble and despair, they trudge back to the jungle, where one of them trips over a moving stick, which turns out to be a python! The captain is impressed and the story ends happily – at least for the crew. The silly humour and crisp, colourful illustrations make this an excellent addition to this series for early readers. **RA 6+/IL 6-8**

Katje the Windmill Cat
Gretchen Woelfle, illustrated by Nicola Bayley
Walker Books ISBN: 0 7445 8939 8 £4.99
This sophisticated picture book marvellously interprets a
traditional Dutch tale, based on a true story about a cat and a
little baby who survived the terrible flood of 5th November 1421,
St Elizabeth's Day. Some pages have small vignettes and are
beautifully decorated with representations of blue and white
tiles, reflecting the best tradition of Dutch craftsmanship.
Overall, there are 84 decorated tiles, which simultaneously tell a
story echoing that of the main plot. The illustrations enhance the
vivid sense of danger and desperation portrayed in the tale.
RA 7+/IL 5-8

The Glass Heart
Sally Gardner
Dolphin ISBN: 1 84255 073 X £4.99
Rosie's Granny tells her the tale of the three beautiful
princesses with fragile glass hearts: the eldest dies, the second
suffers from a cracked heart, and the third, and most beautiful,
has to reject all suitors because they don't know anything about
glass. But then her former page, Valentino, who has apprenticed
himself to a glassblower for three years, returns to claim the
woman he loves. This story, originally a nineteenth-century
German tale, has at its heart a moral about taking care of one
another, and is accompanied by exquisite watercolour
illustrations. **RA 8+/IL 6-9**

That's Not Right!
Alan Durant, illustrated by Katharine McEwen
Red Fox (Flying Foxes) ISBN: 0 09 943198 X £3.99
Ellie is very proud of her story about a bug who gets squashed.
However, Fred the woodlouse has a different opinion, and he
and his mate, Mrs Fred, each think they can improve on Ellie's
narrative. Then, the old shoe, who is portrayed as the villain of
their stories, has yet another idea of how the tale should be told.
An excellent early reader to encourage children to experiment
with their storytelling and to look at ideas from more than one
point of view. Humorous and informative, with clear, bright
illustrations which complement the text. **RA 7+/IL 6-9**

Newly Fluent Readers 6-10

This is an exciting stage in the process of learning to read, as children progress from reading each word separately to reading them together to make a sentence and then finally to understanding the story as a whole. Illustrations are still important and print should be bold and clear, but the stories are longer, more demanding and more fulfilling. Nevertheless, many of the books in this section are still ideal for reading aloud.

Illustration by Lynne Chapman, taken from *Into the Lion's Den* by Terry Deary and Lynne Chapman, reproduced by permission of A & C Black

Bob and the House Elves
Emily Rodda, illustrated by Tim Archbold
Bloomsbury ISBN: 0 7475 5529 X £3.99
Bob is a slovenly type and likes the mess he lives in. He is
aghast therefore when he wakes up one day to find his house
has been tidied by elves. Desperate to get rid of them before
his card-playing, pizza-munching mates arrive on Saturday
evening, he searches in vain for an answer, until at last a
solution presents itself, and love beckons for a reformed Bob. A
lovely, light-hearted story for the younger age group, with some
great running gags, and a satisfying ending. **RA 7+/IL 6-9**

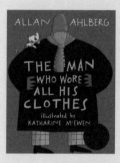

The Man Who Wore All His Clothes
Allan Ahlberg, illustrated by Katharine McEwen
Walker Books ISBN: 0 7445 8995 9 £6.99
This is the first book in a series about the rather unusual
Gaskitt family. Mr Gaskitt works as Father Christmas in a
department store, his wife is a taxi driver and Horace, their cat,
loves spending much of his time watching sad old movies on TV,
lazing around, drinking tea and visiting friends. In this particular
tale, Mrs Gaskitt is caught up in a bank robbery. The colourful
illustrations are an integral part of this hilarious tale. An ideal
book for confident early readers. **RA 7+/IL 6-9**

What Planet Are You From Clarice Bean?
Lauren Child
Orchard Books ISBN: 1 84121 104 4 £4.99
This is a lively and entertaining book. Every single space is
covered with cartoon-like drawings, bright colours, interesting
photographic collage and adventurous typography. Clarice Bean
can't think of a subject for her project on the environment, until
her usually inert brother, Kurt, dashes in, and declares that he is
going to become an eco-warrior and protest against the cutting
down of a very old tree. The family joins, in making posters and
sitting in the tree. Clarice Bean is late again for school, but at
least she's done her project! **RA 7+/IL 6-9**

Pa Jinglebob:
The Fastest Knitter in the West
Mary Arrigan, illustrated by Korky Paul
Egmont (Red Bananas) ISBN: 0 7497 4867 2 £3.99
This hilarious tale is set in the dusty Wild West town of Buckaroo. Jemima Jinglebob is very proud of her Pa, but finds his hobby – knitting! – rather embarrassing. When Not-Nice Nellie and her bandits storm into town, Pa Jinglebob is appointed Sheriff, but the townsfolk are angry when, instead of fighting her, he allows her to throw them all down a well, while the brigands run riot in the saloon. However, Pa Jinglebob has a plan, and uses his skills to knit a giant web to trap the bandits. Short chapters and speech bubbles make this an excellent early reader, and the lively, colourful illustrations provide much entertainment, while underlining the message that violence doesn't solve problems. **RA 7+/IL 6-9**

Fire Cat
Pippa Goodhart, illustrated by Philip Hurst
Egmont (Red Go Bananas) ISBN: 1 4052 0130 4 £3.99
A great fire is raging in London when John meets his father's friend Mr Samuel Pepys, who encourages him to keep a diary of this momentous event. Then John's beloved cat Sammy disappears, so, despite the danger, he sets out to find him amid scenes of devastation and destruction. All ends well in this beautifully illustrated story of the Great Fire of London of 1666, and there are enough facts and activities to keep the reader engaged. **RA 7+/IL 6-9**

Falling Angels
Colin Thompson
Red Fox ISBN: 0 09 943298 6 £5.99
Sally could fly before she could crawl – in fact, we could all fly once, but when you lose your dreams you lose the ability to fly. Sally and her grandmother never lost their dreams, and they use the gift of flight to travel to every corner of the world and explore magical and exciting places. This touching fantasy is perfectly complemented by superbly surreal illustrations which, on their own, would keep a child (or adult) absorbed for hours. A complex and fascinating choice for youngsters. **RA 7+/IL 6-10**

Clottus and the Ghostly Gladiator
Ann Jungman, illustrated by Mike Phillips
A & C Black ISBN: 0 7136 5958 0 £4.99

Clottus and his family are very fond of their favourite slave, Gorjus, but when they hit hard times they have to sell him. Gorjus is distraught and runs away just as the family find out they can keep him after all. Dejected, they visit the new circus nearby, and Clottus thinks there is something very familiar about the gladiator, who is about to be killed. Can Clottus save the day and reunite the family? With black-and-white line drawings throughout, this is an entertaining and informative story of domestic life in Roman Britain. **RA 7+/IL 6-9**

Fierce Milly and the Demon Saucepan
Marilyn McLaughin, illustrated by Leonie Shearing
Egmont ISBN: 1 4052 0064 2 £3.99

Fierce Milly has a mind of her own, a cat called Yo-yo Ferguson, and a very vivid imagination. She also loves multiplying, and would desperately like to get a gold star and her 'news' on the board at school. In this hilarious short story collection she gets both, although the gold star is a bribe from her exasperated teacher to stop her reading out her Demon Saucepan story. (The saucepan chops people's heads off with its lid and melts Barbie dolls until they are a puddle of pink plastic.) A witty, original collection, highly recommended for early readers.
RA 7+/IL 6-9

Witch-in-Training: Flying Lessons
Maeve Friel, illustrated by Nathan Reed
Collins ISBN: 0 00 713341 3 £3.99

When Jessica discovers that she's a witch, she has to learn to fly her broomstick. Fortunately, Miss Strega, her witch-teacher, is firm but patient. She guides Jessica through the complexities of moon vaulting, ejecting unwelcome goblins and negotiating a passage through the very busy Milky Way, until finally Jessica is ready to take her flying test. If she passes, she will become a GASP of BR(EATH) – a Graduate Airborne Spinner and Pilot of Broom Riders (Earth And The Heavens). The witty writing and lively illustrations help to make this a fun book for confident early readers. **RA 7+/IL 6-10**

Notso Hotso
Anne Fine, illustrated by Tony Ross
Puffin ISBN: 0 14 131250 5 £3.99
Anthony, a very vain dog, is horrified when his fur starts to fall out in clumps. On a humiliating trip to the vet, his body is shaved, leaving only the fur on his head and the tip of his tail, so that he resembles a lion. Naked and embarrassed, he returns home expecting a torrent of abuse from the neighbouring animals, but, to his surprise, nobody recognises him. Anthony makes the most of his new appearance, wreaking revenge on his old enemy – next-door's cat! Expressive illustrations and short chapters make this amusing dogs-eye view of the world ideal for those who are just beginning to read alone.
RA 7+/IL 6-10

Speak Up, Spike!
Franzeska G. Ewart, illustrated by Mark Oliver
Egmont (Yellow Go Bananas) ISBN: 1 4052 0073 1 £3.99
Spike is small and shy and people are always telling him to speak up. To make matters worse, he's afraid of the dark and scary shadow monsters. So when his teacher produces shadow puppets of Rama, Sita and the monster Ravana to celebrate Divali, Spike is terrified! However, by the time his class act out the Hindu legend, Spike has discovered he has a voice loud enough to defeat the scariest monster. A sensitive and engaging story about overcoming childhood fears, complemented by lively, comic illustrations. **RA 7+/IL 7-10**

Atlantis: The Legend of a Lost City
Retold and illustrated by Christina Balit
Frances Lincoln ISBN: 0 7112 1906 0 £5.99
Adapted from Plato's *Timaeus* and *Critias*, this is a retelling of the legend of Atlantis: Poseidon wreaks a terrible revenge on the inhabitants of the island utopia he has created when they take up arms against each other. This is a beautifully illustrated book, in which Balit's distinctive style works well with her own text to summon up the magic and mystery of the ancient tale of Atlantis. **RA 7+/IL 7-10**

Into the Lion's Den
Terry Deary, illustrated by Lynne Chapman
A & C Black ISBN: 0 7136 6190 9 £4.99

In ancient Rome, Agnes and her fellow Christians are to be thrown into the amphitheatre to face Max, 'a lion with a nasty temper and bad breath'. Lucilla, the Emperor's spoilt daughter, is keen to see lots of bloodshed on her first trip to the games, but may well get more than she bargained for, as there is a plot afoot to kill her father, the Emperor Marcus Aurelius. The hero of the tale is Cass, a reluctant animal keeper, who attempts to foil the conspirators and save Agnes during a big day at the Colosseum. This funny, well-told story has a good sense of history, short chapters and humorous black-and-white line illustrations. **RA 8+/IL 7-10**

Mister Skip
Michael Morpurgo, illustrated by Griff
Collins ISBN: 0 00 713474 6 £3.99

In this modern fantasy/fairy-tale Jackie and her mum live on an estate surrounded by tower blocks, but dream of a better life in the countryside. Although Jackie looks after Gran's tatty old donkey, Barnaby, she longs, like the local boys, to have her own horse. When she finds an old broken gnome in a skip and lovingly restores him as a birthday present for her mum, her fortunes start to change. Naming the gnome Mister Skip, Jackie confides her fears, hopes and dreams in him – and is stunned when one day he replies! Mister Skip has a way of making things happen and soon the lives of Jackie and her family are transformed beyond their wildest dreams. Short chapters and delightful illustrations make this novel ideal for newly-confident readers. **RA 8+/IL 7-10**

So What!
Bel Mooney, illustrated by Margaret Chamberlain
Egmont ISBN: 0 7497 4823 0 £3.99

This rather jolly little book offers a series of incidents in the life of 10-year-old Kitty and her family. Problems with homework, room-tidying, and jealousy of a younger sibling, are all dealt with in a fairly light-hearted way, but with sympathy for the difficulties of a child confronting the idea of 'growing up'. The style of text and the illustrations will appeal to quite young readers, and the topics covered could be usefully discussed both in a classroom situation and on a more one-to-one basis. **RA 8+/IL 7-10**

Confident Readers 8-11

Once children have mastered the art of reading for themselves, it is important to build their confidence and keep them equipped with as wide a range of types of story as possible. At this stage they may start to distinguish their favourite authors or genres and want to select their own books. This section includes stories that will challenge and surprise readers, holding their interest right up to the final page.

Illustration by Mike Phillips, taken from *The Green Men of Gressingham* by Philip Ardagh and Mike Phillips, reproduced by permission of Barrington Stoke

Confident Readers 8-11

The Invisible Boy
Hazel Townson, illustrated by Tony Ross
Andersen Press ISBN: 1 84270 105 3 £3.99
When Gary's parents split up, his dad takes him to live at Sheldonsea. Both at home and at his new school nobody seems to notice him and Gary suspects that he is becoming invisible, blaming the 'magic' door-key-on-a-string he has to wear around his neck. Gary decides to run away so that people will notice his absence and search for him, proving that he is still visible. However, he becomes embroiled in a series of extraordinary adventures, involving an alien, a spaceship, and even a dead body in an amusement arcade! All is happily resolved in this witty, fast-paced story centred on the emotional isolation which can follow family break-up. **RA 8+/IL 7-10**

Mark Two
Jeanne Willis, illustrated by Tony Ross
Andersen Press ISBN: 1 84270 110 X £3.99
Whittaker, the witty narrator of this highly amusing tale, relates what happens to his best friend, Mark, as he hits puberty at full pace. Mark is busy practising being surly, smelly and unco-operative, when suddenly Mark Two appears behind him in the mirror! His doppelganger is smart, clean, clever and eager, and sets about reforming Mark One's school and home life with gusto. Desperately, the two friends try to eliminate him before he eliminates Mark One. Or can the two Marks compromise and find a way of living together in harmony? Whittaker's account of the change from boyhood to adolescence is funny and fast-paced and the twist in the tale keeps the reader guessing right to the end. **RA 8+/IL 8-11**

Krazy Kow Saves the World – Well, Almost
Jeremy Strong, illustrated by Nick Sharrartt
Puffin ISBN: 0 14 131374 9 £3.99
Jamie Frink is as surprised as he is delighted when his superhero, Krazy Kow, is chosen to be made into a film. He believes that he will be famous, but as time goes by he realises that Krazy Kow is more important to him than fame. In fact, what he sees of fame and fortune proves deeply unattractive, and in the end he has to take a very difficult, but brave, decision. This amusing, yet at times thought-provoking, story rolls along in an off-the-wall way and is sure to delight young readers.
RA 8+/IL 7-12

Best BOOK
GUIDE

Pirate Diary:
The Journal of Jake Carpenter
Richard Platt, illustrated by Chris Riddell
Walker Books ISBN: 0 7445 9430 8 £6.99
This illustrated diary begins in 1716 and describes the amazing adventures of nine-year-old Jake Carpenter as he joins his uncle as a sailor on the high seas. Soon after they set sail, the ship is captured by pirates and Jake finds himself leading an exciting life on the wrong side of the law. Each page is full of drama, including descriptions of the ship and some of the more unpleasant details of life at sea, such as violent storms and floggings. The magnificent illustrations bring the historically-accurate text to life, which is supplemented by an informative glossary of terms. Overall, this is an atmospheric book which would particularly appeal to reluctant boy readers.
RA 8+/IL 7-12

Big George
Eric Pringle, illustrated by Colin Paine
Bloomsbury ISBN: 0 7475 5544 3 £4.99
Big George – the size of several large trees – crash-lands from outer space into twelfth-century England. Initially, the locals are terrified, but George is befriended by Tilly, the miller's daughter, who helps him to survive ridicule and danger from the angry villagers. In return, George helps save Tilly from a bullying father, who has promised her in marriage to the obnoxious, smelly son of the ghastly Baron Lousewort. Moving along at a galumphing good pace, and covering a satisfyingly wide range of emotions, this is a light-hearted story about friendship, packed with comical characters and bungling baddies. **RA 8+/IL 7-11**

The Bodigulpa
Jenny Nimmo, illustrated by David Roberts
Macmillan (Shock Shop) ISBN: 0 330 39750 8 £3.99
After Daniel's grandmother mysteriously disappears and is presumed dead, grumpy Grandpa Green comes to live with Daniel and his parents. To Daniel's dismay, the bad-tempered old man fills their empty greenhouse with sinister-looking plants. Daniel had planned to turn it into Starship Danmatt 1, but now Grandpa Green won't let him near it. One plant in particular – the Bodigulpa – grows to monster-like proportions, bursting through the greenhouse roof! And when the babysitter and her dog also disappear, Daniel's suspicions about the Bodigulpa's insatiable appetite increase. A chilling story, which saves its most horrifying revelation until the very end. **RA 8+/IL 8-11**

The Last Wolf
Michael Morpurgo, illustrated by Michael Foreman
Corgi Yearling ISBN: 0 440 86507 7 £4.99
When Miya teaches her grandfather how to use a computer, he
decides to trace his family tree online. He makes contact with a
relative in America, who emails him the extraordinary memoirs of
his ancestor, Robbie McLeod, whose childhood was spent in the
embattled Scotland of Bonnie Prince Charlie. Befriending the
orphaned wolf pup of 'the last wolf in Scotland', Robbie realises
that to survive they must find a more permanent home overseas.
The action ranges from the Scottish Highlands to the American
plains, but at its heart lies Robbie's enduring relationship with
the wolf. Powerful illustrations underline this captivating tale of
loyalty and bravery. **RA 8+/IL 7-11**

The Green Men of Gressingham
Philip Ardagh, illustrated by Mike Phillips
Barrington Stoke ISBN: 1 84299 085 3 £4.50
In this humorous twist on Robin Hood, Young Tom is looking
forward to his new life as knight-in-training at his uncle's castle.
But disaster strikes when he is kidnapped en route by the
Green Men – a band of vicious-looking outlaws dressed in
brown (it's cheaper than green), led by a beautiful and
mysterious, masked lady, called Robyn. They plan to hold Tom
hostage and storm the castle, rescuing the innocent villagers
imprisoned there for not paying Lord Dashwood's crippling
taxes. However, things do not go to plan. A funny, well-plotted,
action-packed adventure, with amusing black-and-white
illustrations, expressly aimed at reluctant readers.
RA 7+/IL 7-11

The Lost Thing
Shaun Tan
Lothian ISBN: 0 7344 0388 7 £4.99
While walking along the beach collecting bottle tops, a young
boy comes across the 'Lost Thing', a huge red object with six
legs and many windows and doors. It looks sad, but is quite
friendly, and since it seems to belong to nobody in particular, the
boy takes it home, and the two spend a pleasant day together.
He finally takes it to a special place where many unclaimed
items are left. This is a highly original picture book for older
readers with stunning illustrations. It is a wonderful story to read
alone as the illustrations and the whole design of the book have
many interesting details. **RA 8+/IL 7-13**

Strange Exchange
Pat Thomson
Barn Owl Books ISBN: 1 903015 17 0 £4.99
Pascal seems like a normal French boy when he comes to stay with Mike and his family on an exchange visit. Gradually, however, Mike realises that there is something very different about Pascal – and, in fact, the reader already knows that he is an alien from another world, sent here to learn of Earth's customs and culture. This is a genuinely funny book, which would appeal to a wide audience. Nevertheless, it touches on some serious issues and could be a useful way of introducing a discussion on tolerance, understanding and the meaning of true friendship. **RA 9+/IL 8-12**

The Fall of Fergal
Philip Ardagh, illustrated by David Roberts
Faber and Faber ISBN: 0 571 21521 1 £4.99
This darkly comic tale, the first in the *Unlikely Plot* trilogy, begins with a description of young Fergal McNally falling to his death from a hotel window. The book then charts retrospectively the events leading up to Fergal's untimely death. Le Fay McNally has reached the finals of the national Tap 'n' Type typing competition, which are to be held in the luxurious Dell Hotel. Her siblings want to offer moral support, but – being a bit short of cash – they secretly share her hotel room, raising the suspicions of hotel detective Charlie 'Twinkle-Toes' Tweedy, whose investigation will have fatal consequences. The superb, gothic illustrations, and surreal twists and turns, add to the fun of this highly entertaining story. **RA 9+/IL 8-12**

Toro! Toro!
Michael Morpurgo, illustrated by Michael Foreman
Collins ISBN: 0 00 710718 8 £4.99
Antonio tells his grandson how, as a small boy in 1936, he saved the life of his favourite bull, destined for the bullring, by taking him out into the hills. By doing so, he also saved his own life, when Nazi planes strafed his village, killing his family. Describing the boy's flight to find shelter, Morpurgo gives a graphic account of the hardships of the Spanish Civil War. Readers will empathise with Antonio's story, while acquiring an understanding of a European conflict, which has rarely been the subject of children's literature. **RA 8+/IL 9-11**

Danger by Moonlight
Jamila Gavin, illustrated by David Dean
Egmont ISBN: 0 7497 4886 9 £3.99

Geronimo Veronese is a jeweller who leaves Venice to seek his fortune at the court of the Great Mogul Shah Jehan in Hindustan. Twelve years later his youngest son, Filippo, sets off on a hazardous journey to find the father he has never known. Set in the glittering world of the Ottoman Empire, Filippo's sense of wonder is combined with increasing dread, as he finds himself in a foreign land where nothing is as it seems. Running through the book is the dazzling image of Veronese's masterpiece, a jewelled pendant called The Ocean of the Moon. Although it does not bring Filippo the happiness he longs for, it becomes the inspiration for something far greater – a monument to love, in the form of the Taj Mahal. A sophisticated and colourful tale. **RA 8+/IL 8-12**

Frindle
Andrew Clements
Simon & Schuster ISBN: 0 689 83703 8 £4.99

When Nick's tough-minded old English teacher tells him that users give words their meanings, he invents a new word, 'frindle', to rename what had previously been called a pen. He succeeds in getting the new word adopted throughout his school and further afield, despite Mrs Granger's opposition. In a sense, that is all that happens, but the narration is gripping, and the meanings go deep. This is a brilliantly funny and touching story about education, which ought to give pleasure to teachers as well as pupils. **RA 8+/IL 9-12**

Maggot Pie
Michael Lawrence
Orchard Books ISBN: 1 84121 756 5 £4.99

Jiggy McCue considers himself unlucky and this continues to be the case after he uses the Piddle Pool and finds he is the master of JR the genie. He uses up his three wishes in a thoughtless moment and then he manages to upset the genie who decides he wants to reek revenge on Jiggy, his friends, his school and the local zoo. Lawrence has created another fast-paced plot, which has some good one-liners, riddles and revolting scenarios. This humorous story has plenty of unsavoury incidents, involving maggots and other gross substances, that will undoubtedly appeal to most children! **RA 9+/IL 8-11**

Mighty Fizz Chilla
Philip Ridley, illustrated by Stephen Lee
Puffin ISBN: 0 14 038510 X £4.99
Milo has become a sullen, angry 'monster', so his mum sends
him to stay with an old family friend who lives by the sea. Milo
finds himself drawn into the lives of the wild Captain Jellicoe (a
man even more angry than he is), the obsessive Dee Dee, who
can only tolerate 'Facts', and the blind, loving Cressida. What is
the story that links all their lives? And why will the Captain not
rest until he has hunted down and destroyed the Mighty Fizz
Chilla? In this modern myth, Milo is helped to transform himself
back into a loving son. An energetic, absorbing story, told in an
original, humorous way. **RA 9+/IL 9-12**

'Funny, original, moving' INDEPENDENT ON SUNDAY

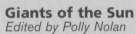

Love That Dog
Sharon Creech
Bloomsbury ISBN: 0 7475 5749 7 £4.99
Jack has a great sadness in his life, but he is not about to share
his feelings with anyone, and he is *definitely* not going to write
poetry about it – he's a boy isn't he? However, intrigued by the
weekly poems his teacher reads to the class, he tentatively
responds. By writing his own poems, Jack begins to explore
feelings of anger and loss, as well as joyful recollections of his
much-loved dog, Sky. Jack is encouraged to invite his favourite
poet to visit the class, and this becomes the turning point in his
return to a rich and exciting world of learning and discovery. This
heart-warming, unusually structured story, which includes the
poems that the teacher uses with the class, resonates long after
the final page. **RA 8+/IL 9-12**

Giants of the Sun
Edited by Polly Nolan
Macmillan ISBN: 0 330 39617 X £4.99
This collection of 14 short stories by Irish writers encompasses
a wide variety of topics, ranging from the seriously thoughtful to
the entertainingly bizarre, and covers everything from bed-
wetting to sparkly eye shadow! Extremely well-written with a
wide-ranging appeal, the collection is suitable for most ages,
although sometimes a little sophisticated for younger children.
The stories are a good length for reading out loud, with useful
potential for group discussion afterwards. **RA 9+/IL 7-12**

Dog
Daniel Pennac, translated by Sarah Adams
Walker Books ISBN: 0 7445 9009 4 £4.99

Dog is abandoned as a puppy because he is ugly, but, fortunately, he is adopted by Black Nose, a bitch who looks out for him and advises him on how to survive the dangers of life on the streets. Following Black Nose's death, and a series of misfortunes, Dog ends up in a pound. Eventually, he is taken home by a family, 'Mr Muscle' and 'Mrs Squeak', and their daughter, Plum. Although Plum is initially very fond of her new pet, she soon loses interest, and Dog has to work hard to train her to care for him. This is a captivating account of the life of a dog, beautifully narrated, full of suspense and a must for all dog lovers! **RA 9+/IL 8-12**

The Wanderings of Odysseus
Retold by Rosemary Sutcliff, illus. by Alan Lee
Frances Lincoln ISBN: 0 7112 1846 3 £8.99

The fantastic voyages of Odysseus, and his battles against gods and monsters, are majestically retold in Rosemary Sutcliff's sequel to *Black Ships Before Troy*. The language, as you would expect from a children's writer of this calibre, is both challenging and captivating, and Homer's epic poem is further brought to life by Alan Lee's magnificent illustrations. There is a glossary at the end of the book to help with the pronunciation of the Greek names, and a map indicating the sites traditionally identified with Odysseus' travels. **RA 9+/IL 8-12**

Ten of the Best
Edited by Wendy Cooling
(short stories by various authors)
Collins ISBN: 0 00 713339 1 £5.99

Ten of today's best children's authors recount a variety of stories from their school days. Michael Morpurgo's account of his boarding school misery is incredibly moving; Malorie Blackman's recollections of victimisation in the playground will be familiar to many readers; and Bernard Ashley's experiences as an evacuee schoolboy in Preston provide a fascinating historical snapshot. With hilarious and revealing contributions from Paul Jennings, Jeremy Strong, Berlie Doherty, Jenny Nimmo, Margaret Mahy, Michael Rosen and Robert Swindells, this collection of short stories is fascinating and highly recommended. **RA 9+/IL 8-12**

Able Readers 10-12

At this stage most young readers enjoy the challenge and diversity that good fiction presents. The books in this section cover an intriguing variety of subjects and encourage readers to turn their imagination to more demanding stories.

Illustration copyright © David Frankland, 2001, taken from *Mortal Engines* by Philip Reeve, first published by Scholastic Children's Books, reproduced by permission of Scholastic Ltd

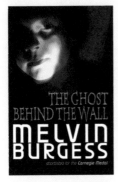

The Ghost Behind the Wall
Melvin Burgess
Puffin ISBN: 0 14 131027 8 £4.99

12-year-old David is bullied by his peers and is constantly in trouble. When he discovers a network of ventilation shafts running behind the walls throughout his block of flats, he feels compelled to explore. However, he is petrified when confronted by the ghost of a young boy who seems intent on terrorising old Mr Alveston, a resident suffering from Alzheimer's disease. As well as being a spooky ghost story, this multi-layered novel is also a touching and honest look at the frustrations of Alzheimer's disease, and explores the moving friendship that develops between David and Mr Alveston. **RA 9+/IL 9-12**

Bambert's Book of Missing Stories
Reinhardt Jung, translated by Anthea Bell, illustrated by Peter Allen
Egmont ISBN: 0 7497 4705 6 £4.99

In a small Austrian town, Bambert lives as a recluse above the grocery shop of his kindly tenant, Mr Bloom. He spends his time writing stories and sends ten of them away by Japanese hot-air balloons to foreign countries, planning to rewrite them when they return, so that they fit the lands they have reached. The eleventh story he leaves totally blank, for the recipient to invent. This is an exceptional book. It appears at first to be a set of fairy tales, yet each story has a relevance to the life of its author, and all are set within the encompassing relationship between Bambert and Bloom. This results in a magical, multi-layered tale, which will delight readers of all ages. **RA 9+/IL 9-12**

Tongue-Tied!
Paul Jennings
Puffin ISBN: 0 14 038511 8 £4.99

Paul Jennings' stories aren't just funny, or scary, or stomach-churningly disgusting (although they are all these things): they have a way of getting under your skin, touching a nerve, and inspiring deep thoughts about things you might never have bothered with before. In this collection, 'Sniffex' helps find the Phantom Farter of class 6B, hailstone bugs are bred to finance a magic show, and a pair of ancient spectacles are used to get in touch with the ghost world. Zany and twisted, yet thought-provoking, this collection makes compulsive reading.
RA 10+/IL 9-13

The Amazing Maurice and His Educated Rodents
Terry Pratchett
Corgi ISBN: 0 552 54693 3 £5.99

After consuming the remains of a magical potion, a group of rats and a street-wise cat called Maurice become incredibly intelligent. Maurice masterminds an ingenious money-making scheme whereby they travel across the land with a 'stupid-looking kid who plays a pipe'. Pied-piper style, the boy rids each town of the 'plague of vermin', and is handsomely rewarded. However, when they reach the town of Bad Blintz, they all get more than they bargained for. A witty fantasy adventure, with a wonderful variety of characters, this superficially frivolous tale, actually raises some serious points about the nature of friendship, society and greed. **RA 9+/IL 9-13**

Rocket Science
Jeanne Willis
Faber and Faber ISBN: 0 571 21275 1 £4.99

Adam Lurie is gifted, friendless, and has a passion for all things extra-terrestrial. When a strange creature turns up on the beach near his home, it doesn't take much to convince him he has found an alien. While hiding the 'alien' from the outside world, Adam hatches a plan to return him to his own planet – by building a rocket. This book contains a fair amount of technical data about rocket building and has a wonderfully poignant ending in which we come to understand the true identity of the alien. A well-balanced, well-written story, which explores the nature of family relationships and friendship. **RA 10+/IL 9-13**

Fox
Matthew Sweeney, illus. by Christopher Corr
Bloomsbury ISBN: 0 7475 6040 4 £5.99

Gerard is a loner who has just moved to the city. Exploring the new neighbourhood on his bike he becomes fascinated by a homeless man with a pet fox. As he struggles to cope with his unfamiliar surroundings, Gerard withdraws into his own world, where only his drawing and his fragile relationship with the man and his fox give him confidence. Gerard's narration of the story, and the drawings that accompany it, make this a very personal journey, in which Matthew Sweeney succeeds in drawing attention to the homeless – 'who they are, how they live and what they mean in this world'. **RA 8+/IL 10-13**

Midnight for Charlie Bone
Jenny Nimmo
Egmont ISBN: 0 7497 4888 5 £4.99

Charlie is unnerved to discover that he can hear people in photographs talking. His aunts take an unhealthy interest in his gift and send him to the notorious Bloor's Academy, where he meets other children with 'endowments' (magical powers). What happened to the girl in the photograph and why is everyone so interested in the metal case Charlie has been given to look after? Charlie and his friends will need all their wits about them if they are to unravel the mystery before it is too late. This gripping and imaginative fantasy has a fascinating cast of characters. A tantalising 'to be continued' at the end of the book will leave readers desperate for more. **RA 10+/IL 10-12**

Pumpkin Pie
Jean Ure, illustrated by Karen Donnelly
Collins ISBN: 0 00 714392 3 £3.99

Jenny has a loving family, but they never really find time to communicate with each other. Mum is a high-flying career woman, dad is a househusband and part-time chef, her gorgeous older sister is boy mad and her younger brother is a child genius. When Jenny and her best friend, Saffy, start drama classes, Jenny's confidence is knocked when she is told that she should lose weight if she wants to be a star. She becomes obsessed with food and gradually becomes bulimic, which she successfully hides from her preoccupied family. There are lots of serious issues discussed in this book, but overall, it is a very funny, light-hearted read, which provides an excellent basis for discussion with young adolescents. **RA 9+/IL 10-12**

Dovey Coe
Frances O'Roark Dowell
Walker Books ISBN: 0 7445 9029 9 £4.99

Set in the sleepy mountain town of Indian Creek, North Carolina, this tale is narrated by 12-year-old Dovey Coe. It is no secret that headstrong Dovey dislikes wealthy Parnell Caraway, who spends the summer courting her beautiful sister, Caroline, and taunting her deaf brother, Amos. When Parnell is murdered, Dovey is the obvious suspect, but with the aid of an inexperienced young lawyer from the city, she struggles to prove her innocence. This powerfully-written novel is full of suspense and strongly evokes the sights and sounds of 1920s America. **RA 9+/IL 10-12**

Saffy's Angel
Hilary McKay
Hodder Children's Books ISBN: 0 340 85080 9 £5.99
Families don't come much stranger than Saffron's. The children are all named after paints on a colour chart, their mother spends the majority of her time locked in the garden shed, and the family house (inexplicably named 'Banana House') is teeming with guinea pigs. Saffron found out a few years ago that her brother and sisters are actually her cousins (her real mother died when she was small), but it is her grandfather's death that suddenly triggers distant memories. Aided by her wheelchair-using neighbour, Saffy starts to investigate. An uplifting story about an eccentric family encased in chaos, but also full of intense warmth and loyalty. **RA 9+/IL 9-13**

War Games
Jenny Koralek
Egmont ISBN: 1 4052 0074 X £4.99
Set during the Second World War, this is a tale of an enduring friendship, that develops between two young children. Hugo, a Jewish refugee, is whisked away from his family in Prague just before the Nazis invade. He speaks no English, and understands little of what is happening around him. Holly's family abandon their life in South Africa to return to England, but Holly desperately misses the only home she remembers. The two children cling together throughout the war, as they grow towards puberty and a final separation. This is a moving account of childhood in a dark and stressful time, and explores family feeling and friendship. **RA 9+/IL 10-12**

My Girragundji
Meme McDonald and Boori Pryor
Allen & Unwin ISBN: 1 86448 818 2 £4.99
Growing up is never easy, but when racists and bullies pick fights with you, the grown-ups argue all the time, your seven sisters poke fun at you and, worst of all, there's a bad, ugly, stinky Hairyman in your house just waiting to get you when your guard is down, things can't get much worse. However, when you have a friend to give you courage, bullies don't seem so big – and what better friend than Girragundji, a little, green, tree frog. Based on the real life experiences of one of the authors and his family, this fascinating story gives a rare insight into growing up between two worlds, and rites of passage in Aboriginal culture. A most unusual book, illustrated throughout with black and white drawings and photographs. **RA 9+/IL 9-12**

Jake's Tower
Elizabeth Laird
Macmillan ISBN: 0 330 39803 2 £4.99
Jake lives a dismal life with his mother and Steve, his extremely violent stepfather. His only refuge is his imagination and he dreams of living in a secluded tower on an island, where nobody can hurt him. After a particularly vicious beating, his mother flees in desperation to Mrs Judd, Jake's paternal grandmother, whom he has never met. Gradually, they get to know each other, and Jake is overwhelmed when he meets his real father for the first time – although he is not quite what he had imagined. This short novel admirably tackles the difficult subject of domestic violence, and Jake is a brave, convincing character, full of maturity and passion. **RA 10+/IL 9-12**

Stop the Train
Geraldine McCaughrean
Oxford University Press ISBN: 0 19 275266 9 £4.99
This novel is set in 1890s Oklahoma. Cissy's family buys a plot of land in Florence, hoping to build a new life there. However, when the newly settled residents anger the railroad company by refusing to sell them some of their land, the train will no longer stop in Florence. Without supplies and tourism, the town cannot flourish and the community struggles to survive, so everyone desperately tries to think of a way to stop the train. This is a very satisfying novel, with an exciting plot that thoroughly engages the reader, and the wealth of characters are a joy.
RA 10+/IL 9-12

Journey to the River Sea
Eva Ibbotson
Macmillan ISBN: 0 330 39715 X £4.99
This satisfyingly old-fashioned story is set in the early 1900s. Orphan Maia is thrilled to learn she is to live with relatives in South America. She cannot wait to experience the sights, sounds and smells of the Amazon and is particularly looking forward to meeting her twin cousins. When Maia arrives, however, the unpleasant family are far from welcoming and she is saddened to see that the Carter family have blocked out all evidence of the rainforest from their stuffy home. Maia turns to her strict yet kindly governess, Miss Minton, for company, and strikes up some unusual and rewarding friendships. This exciting Amazonian adventure is a compelling read. **RA 10+/IL 9-12**

Artemis Fowl
Eoin Colfer
Puffin ISBN: 0 14 131212 2 £4.99
Artemis Fowl is a twelve-year-old criminal mastermind, who
hatches an ingenious plot to steal all the gold in fairy land, aided
by his loyal bodyguard, Butler. But they have not bargained for
elf Holly Short, who as the first female officer in the Lower
Elements Police Reconnaissance unit (or LEPrecon) has much
to prove. When they kidnap her, she is determined to stand her
ground and protect the fairy secrets. Although incredibly
unscrupulous, Artemis is an extremely likeable protagonist, and
the explanations of the structure and technology of fairy land
are completely believable, making this an action-packed,
amusing and imaginative fairy adventure. **RA 10+/IL 9-12**

Finding Sophie
Irene N. Watts
Floris Books ISBN: 0 86315 374 7 £4.99
Fourteen-year-old Sophie has lived happily with 'Aunt Em' since
she was evacuated from Berlin in 1938. She can no longer
speak German and has become totally immersed in British life
and culture. However, as the Second World War draws to a
close, she begins to wonder about the fate of her Jewish father
and Aryan mother. When she receives a letter from her father,
she fears that she will have to return to Germany and to another
life in an unknown country. The sequel to *Goodbye Marianne*
and *Remember Me* is a compelling conclusion to a moving
trilogy. **RA 10+/IL 10-13**

The Tiger Rising
Kate DiCamillo
Walker Books ISBN: 0 7445 8964 9 £3.99
For Rob, finding the tiger in the woods is miraculous. After his
mother's funeral he becomes master of the art of not thinking
about things – especially at school where he is horribly bullied.
Things start to change when Robert meets Sistine: eccentric,
stubborn and very angry, Sistine doesn't believe in keeping quiet.
She encourages Rob to say his mother's name out loud and
when Rob shares his secret tiger with her, a time approaches
when both he and his father must learn to let go. Kate
DiCamillo is a poetic writer, whose simple tale carries a universal
theme. In struggling to free the tiger in the woods, Rob and
Sistine are forced to take responsibility for themselves and
confront the dangers of keeping things locked up inside for too
long. **RA 10+/IL 10-13**

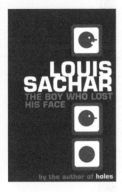

The Boy Who Lost His Face
Louis Sachar
Bloomsbury ISBN: 0 7475 5528 1 £4.99

Desperate to be accepted by the 'in-crowd', David helps to steal old Mrs Bayfield's cane, but is immediately wracked with guilt. When everything in his life starts to go wrong, he becomes convinced that Mrs Bayfield has put a curse on him. He is taunted by his classmates, and his best friend, Scott, makes fun of him to gain popularity with the bullies. To make matters worse, he is smitten with classmate Tori Williams, but unable to ask her out in case the curse strikes again. Luckily, his new friends, Larry and Mo, are on hand to help him confront the bullies and overcome the 'curse'. This is a funny, thought-provoking insight into the mind of an anxious teenager. David is an immensely likeable protagonist and his relationships with family, friends and enemies are thoroughly convincing.
RA 10+/IL 10-12

Stella
Catherine R. Johnson
Oxford University Press ISBN: 0 19 275231 6 £4.99

Stella is a performing clairvoyant in nineteenth-century London. When her beloved guardian, Nana, dies unexpectedly, Stella relies on their savings to keep her alive. She is horrified to discover that Nana's brother, the Reverend Morris, and banker Mr Evans have conspired to swindle her out of her money, knowing that as a mixed-race orphan she has no real chance of challenging them. However, Stella is a resourceful girl and together with her friend Thomas, the undertaker's assistant, she embarks on an adventure that will yield surprising discoveries and a few real ghosts. This racy tale spins a good yarn, and brings Victorian London vividly to life. **RA 10+/IL 10-12**

Lawlor's Revenge
Mary Arrigan
Collins ISBN: 0 00 713765 6 £4.99

Teenager Bron becomes worried when an old lady she has befriended says that she has started seeing and hearing things. Then she just disappears. This fast-moving story follows Bron's pursuit of justice through time as she helps Alby, a ghost from the 1800s, change the course of history for his family. There is plenty of action, adventure, and some chilling moments to hold the reader. The two narrative strands are brought together at the end in a clever last sentence. **RA 10+/IL 10-13**

Parvana's Journey
Deborah Ellis

Oxford University Press ISBN: 0 19 275285 5 £4.99

In this sequel to *The Breadwinner*, 13-year-old Parvana has to dress as a boy to enable her to work in Taliban-controlled Afghanistan. After her father dies, she drifts alone across the ravaged country in search of the remainder of her family, but is not alone for long. Her generous nature leads her to acquire a just-weaned baby, a bad-tempered, disabled boy, and an eight-year-old girl with a disastrous survival technique. A moving story, with a deeply satisfying ending, the novel convincingly portrays the story of the real children behind the headlines about landmines and refugee camps. **RA 10+/IL 9-14**

Gathering Blue
Lois Lowry

Bloomsbury ISBN: 0 7475 5592 3 £5.99

This fantasy tale is set in a future where harshness and cruelty are the norm. Recently-orphaned Kira must learn to survive alone in this bleak environment, but her life is made more difficult by a disability which is not tolerated in her society. She struggles to earn a living, until she realises she has a gift that changes her life forever. The reader encounters a repulsive society, peopled by humans who show no compassion and no love – not even for the children. Only near the end does Kira learn that things do not have to be like this, when she hears of a place where people are caring and show kindness to one another. A very thought-provoking read, which should appeal to children beginning to take an interest in the wider world.
RA 10+/IL 11-14

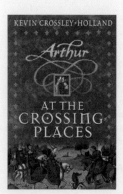

Arthur: At the Crossing Places
Kevin Crossley-Holland

Orion ISBN: 1 84255 200 7 £5.99

This second instalment in the *Arthur* trilogy is set in 1200 on the English-Welsh borderland. Arthur, now aged 14, leaves Caldicot and his childhood behind to take up a position as squire to Lord Stephen. Finding his feet in a new environment, he has to negotiate several awkward situations at the manor while making preparations to accompany Lord Stephen on Crusade. He also continues to follow the adventures of King Arthur and his Knights in his 'seeing stone'. Written in bite-sized chapters, the sharpness of the writing is as effective as ever, setting the stage for a gripping conclusion to the trilogy in *Arthur: King of the Middle March*. **RA 11+/IL 10-14**

The Devil's Toenail
Sally Prue
Oxford University Press ISBN: 0 19 271911 4 £6.99
Horrific bullying has left Stevie permanently disfigured and full
of fear and self-loathing. When he finds an ancient fossil on the
beach, he convinces himself it has magical, dark powers and
can make his life better. But after a series of traumatic, terrifying
events, Stevie finally realises that the only one who can make
the changes is himself. This cleverly-constructed story unfolds
layer upon layer of revelations about Stevie and the mental
scars hidden beneath his physical disfigurement. Full of
suspense, it is a masterful examination of the nature of good
and evil. **RA 10+/IL 10-14**

Malka
Marjam Pressler
Young Picador ISBN: 0 330 41550 6 £9.99
Malka's childhood is shattered when the Germans begin their
'operations' and she has to escape across the border to
Hungary with her mother and sister. When she is separated
from them and arrives back in Poland, she learns to survive
alone in the Jewish ghetto, in a climate of fear and danger,
while her desperate mother struggles to find her. A powerful,
haunting tale, based on a true story, which explores the survival
dilemmas faced by Jews living under occupation in the 1940s.
RA 10+/IL 10-14

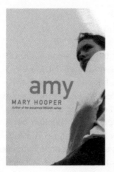

Amy
Mary Hooper
Bloomsbury ISBN: 0 7475 5694 6 £5.99
An extremely topical story about the dangers of internet
chatrooms and date-rape drugs. The book is written as a
transcript of Amy's recorded account to the police of the events
leading up to her date with a boy she has met through the
internet, and includes their email conversations. Although the
denouement is not as serious as it could be, the book highlights
the dangers of chatroom dating and contains some very sound
advice about how to use the internet sensibly, and how to avoid
getting into a situation like Amy's. **RA 10+/IL 10-14**

Holly Starcross
Berlie Doherty
Puffin ISBN: 0 14 037953 3 £3.99
Holly Starcross is having an identity crisis. She lives with her mum, Henry (her mother's partner) and her half-brother and sisters. She has a great best friend and a crush on the cutest boy in the school, but she keeps finding herself asking the question 'Who am I?' When her long lost father turns up out of the blue, Holly is forced to face up to her past and reassess her future. This is a beautifully told story about the confusion of growing up and the pain caused by family separation and torn loyalties. **RA 10+/IL 10-14**

The Edge
Alan Gibbons
Dolphin ISBN: 1 84255 094 2 £4.99
Danny and his mother Cathy are on the run from her abusive boyfriend, Chris. They go back to the Edge, Cathy's childhood home, which she left after having Danny at the age of sixteen. Although Danny's grandmother is happy to see them, his grandfather is reluctant to accept him because he is black, and Danny soon realises that many people in the Edge share his grandfather's racist views. However, Danny is not willing to give up his hope for a new life, and his struggle to make the Edge his home starts to bear fruit. Unfortunately, Chris does not give up so easily and events reach a violent climax. This hard-hitting page-turner targets violence of two kinds – domestic and racist – and emphasises the importance of standing up to aggressors. **RA 10+/IL 10-14**

Cold Tom
Sally Prue
Oxford University Press ISBN: 0 19 271887 8 £6.99
Tom has always lived with the Tribe, a group of elves who are beautifully graceful, yet harsh and unforgiving, and do not tolerate weakness. He has always believed that he is one of them, but as he gets older, he realises that compared to them, his voice is ugly, and he is clumsy and slow. He flees for his life when he senses they are turning against him and hides among the 'demons' (humans) in the city. Although they repulse him, he finds himself increasingly drawn to one in particular, Anna. Much to his disgust and fear, she tries to befriend him and binds him to her with a force that he has never experienced before – friendship. This is a compelling, imaginative novel with more than a hint of magic. **RA 10+/IL 11-14**

Stop Pretending
Sonya Sones
Orion ISBN: 1 84255 075 6 £4.99

Cookie's big sister is intelligent, articulate, beautiful and funny, but suddenly, one Christmas Eve, she has a severe mental breakdown. Through a series of haunting poems, Cookie explores her own feelings of loss, loneliness, guilt, anger and frustration over her sister's condition, the effect it has on the rest of the family and the reactions of other people. This stunningly original 'novel in verse' draws on the author's real-life experiences and is a moving, uplifting and brutally honest story with a positive ending. **RA 9+/IL 11+**

Mortal Engines
Philip Reeve
Scholastic (Point) ISBN: 0 439 97943 9 £5.99

This exciting novel offers action, romance, mystery, revenge, crime and horror. Tom, a Londoner, can't imagine a life not on the move, as the traction city of London trawls the world on wheels, capturing and eating smaller towns and cities. That is, until he is thrown off London by his childhood hero Valentine, with the mysterious Hester, and is forced to reassess life as he knows it. Packed full of colourful characters and locations, this is a whirlwind adventure that challenges both Tom and the reader's attitudes. **RA 11+/IL 11+**

The Sight
David Clement-Davies
Macmillan ISBN: 0 330 48385 4 £6.99

This epic saga begins with the birth of two wolf cubs, Fell and Larka, in the Carpathian Mountains in Transylvania. The reader is led into the enthralling, dark and dangerous world of a family of wolves, for whom the belief in Wolfbane (a demon spirit) and the Sight (the gift of seeing the future or truth), proves as dangerous as other rival packs of wolves, predators and the ferocious elements. This tale has rich layers of myth and philosophy, which constantly encourage the reader to reflect on fundamental human beliefs. This is a long and challenging read, but an intensely rewarding and thought-provoking story for more able readers. **RA 11+/IL 11+**

Adventurous Readers 12+

There is often little to distinguish many teenage books from adult fiction and many adventurous young readers may already be scanning the adult shelves in search of a thrilling story. The subjects covered in this section are often intellectually and emotionally challenging and help young people to develop understanding, maturity and judgement.

Illustration by Rian Hughes, taken from *Never Ever* by Helena Pielichaty, reproduced by permission of Oxford University Press

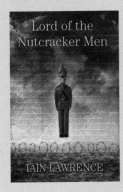

Lord of the Nutcracker Men
Iain Lawrence
Collins ISBN: 0 00 713557 2 £4.99

For his ninth birthday Johnny's father carves him a wonderful army of nutcracker soldiers, and even after he's been called up to fight against the Kaiser, he continues to send Johnny toy soldiers wrapped in letters describing his 'great adventure' in France. But, gradually and chillingly, both letters and wooden toys begin to reveal the truth about this 'war to end all wars'. Is that soldier sleeping or dead? Is this one digging trenches, or graves? As Johnny engages his toy soldiers in increasingly bloody battles, he starts to believe that in some nightmarish way his father's fate is entangled with the figures, and his life is literally in Johnny's hands. This poignant and powerful story is a reminder of the horror of war and its devastating and far-reaching effects on people's lives. **RA 11+/IL 11+**

Feather Boy
Nicky Singer
Collins ISBN: 0 00 712026 5 £4.99

Robert is having a tough time at school, being bullied by Nicker; he's also trying to deal with the break-up of his parents' marriage. He feels that it's just his luck to be landed with a 'spooky old bat' called Edith, when his class takes part in a project with the local old people's home. However, in attempting to solve the mystery of her son's death, he confronts both his bully and his own fears. The reader is drawn through the novel by some wonderfully-moving moments of humour, tension and sadness. **RA 11+/IL 12-14**

Dancing in My Nuddy-Pants
Louise Rennison
Piccadilly Press ISBN: 1 85340 736 4 £6.99

Angst-ridden teenage heroine, Georgia Nicolson, hilariously reflects on the trials, tribulations and occasional delights of adolescence, recorded in minute-by-minute diary form. This fourth book in the series sees Georgia suffering her usual problems with boys and school, continuing her on/off relationships with the Sex God and Dave the Laugh, and enduring the embarrassing behaviour of her parents. But despite her casual talk of 'red-bottomosity', 'trouser snake addendums', and of course, 'nuddy-pants', she is in fact a very moral and restrained teenager – the only unplanned pregnancy in the book is the one bestowed by Georgia's cat, Angus, on Naomi, the kitten next door! **RA 11+/IL 11-15**

Slaves of the Mastery
William Nicholson
Egmont ISBN: 0 7497 4901 6 £5.99
In this second volume of the *Wind on Fire* trilogy, Kestrel is separated from her family when the soldiers of the Mastery destroy the city of Aramanth and take its people into slavery. She vows to find the enemy and take revenge for what has happened. Held captive in the High Domain, the Manth people are subjected to the true horror of the Mastery. When Bowman meets a stranger in the night, he starts to learn the powers of the Singer people and begins to come to terms with his destiny. Only when the Mastery has been destroyed will the Manth people be free to seek their homeland. This is a thrilling and complex fantasy which brings to life in terrifying detail a time of abject cruelty. **RA 11+/IL 12+**

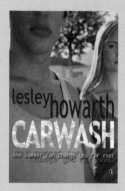

Carwash
Lesley Howarth
Puffin ISBN: 0 14 131079 0 £4.99
Luke is looking forward to reopening his carwash business over the summer, while his brother Danny worries that their dad will discover he has broken the new quad bike. Their neighbour Bix is recovering from glandular fever, and can't figure out what is wrong with Liv, her gorgeous and popular sister, who is behaving strangely since she broke up with her sleazy boyfriend. This novel doesn't have an action-packed plot; in fact, very little happens. The author's main interest is in the subtle ways in which the teenage characters grow up just a little bit more during one summer. The depiction and understanding of their world and language is admirable. **RA 11+/IL 12+**

The Haunting of Alaizabel Cray
Chris Wooding
Scholastic (Point) ISBN: 0 439 99452 7 £5.99
London is under attack, and after dark people don't dare to go south of the River Thames for fear of wolves, murderers and the terrifying wych-kin, who prey on the vulnerable. Thaniel Fox is a wych-hunter, a dangerous job, which becomes even more so, after he finds the elusive Alaizabel Cray, a lost girl who remembers nothing of her past life. In a time when one small mistake can kill, can Thaniel solve Alaizabel's secret before it finishes him off? A truly dark and scary story that keeps you gripped all the way through. **RA 12+/IL 12+**

You Don't Know Me
David Klass
Puffin ISBN: 0 14 131406 0 £5.99
John is a fourteen-year-old American, whose life is a catalogue
of disasters, many of which will be familiar to readers. Because
of his parents' split, and the abuse he suffers from his mother's
new partner, John distances reality by fantasising, and by
denying the existence of everything he fears and hates, before a
final violent episode with his abuser resolves his trauma. A
searingly funny, challenging book, in both style and content, with
enormous potential for use in PSHE and Literacy.
RA 11+/IL 12+

The Ship That Fell Like a Star
Anne Lewis
Honno ISBN: 1 870206 51 7 £5.99
This saga begins on a space station above the planet Antor,
where two children, Zak and Vinny, discover a secret breeding
programme. The tale then moves forward several hundred years,
to find descendants of the children fighting a dictatorship.
Moving back again to Antor, the tale continues, connected by
the story of Mump and Diggory. The children are forced on a
journey in which they fight monsters and the deadly Krais,
assisted by the giant Thalans – but some of them are playing a
traitorous game. This is a gripping story, rich in imagination,
language and characterisation. **RA 12+/IL 12+**

Starry Nights
Judith Clarke
Allen & Unwin ISBN: 1 86508 604 5 £5.99
The Sinclair family are not happy. Jess thought a move to the
country was supposed to make things better, but Mum is still ill,
and lies silent and uncommunicative upstairs. Even lively, funny
Vida has become spiteful, superstitious and moody and Clem's
boxes remain untouched in his room. When she first becomes
aware of a ghostly presence, Jess is afraid things will become
worse still, but perhaps this spirit from beyond the grave holds
the key to the family's return to normal life. A cleverly-
constructed mystery/ghost story that will keep you guessing
until the very end. **RA 11+/IL 12+**

From Out of the Shadows
Jamila Gavin
Egmont ISBN: 1 4052 0280 7 £4.99
These eight short stories for teenagers are beautifully told. The canvas is wide and the collection embraces science fiction, realism, and fantasy: a brother and sister take their chances in the desert of a dying world; a boy becomes a fox; an Asian girl disgraces her parents; a ghost drummer boy from the English Civil War seeks his drum over the centuries. The language is rich, colourful and compelling; the characters varied and full of feeling. Each story is a gem. **RA 11+/IL 12+**

Match of Death
James Riordan
Oxford University Press ISBN: 0 19 271879 7 £6.99
Fifteen-year-old Vova lives for his football. However, when the Nazis invade the Ukraine in 1941, he is forced to change his priorities, as life becomes a desperate and bloody fight for survival. When the Nazis challenge the Ukraines to the ultimate game of football, Vova must decide whether he is willing to win – and therefore die – for his country. This is a gritty and thought-provoking read, based on true events, that took place during the Second World War. Dramatic, moving, but also highly readable, the book does not shy away from the harsh realities of war. **RA 11+/IL 13+**

Never Ever
Helena Pielichaty
Oxford University Press ISBN: 0 19 275261 8 £4.99
Erin has never seen herself as a snob, but when her father is made bankrupt and they have to move to a council estate, she is not happy. Now, as well as sharing classrooms with the 'yobs', she also has to get the same bus as the airhead girls she despises, and Liam, who fancies himself too much. But everything on the estate is more complex than she realises. Liam's family is rich because his father – who is illiterate – is a brilliant businessman, and his best friend, Tommo, is being physically abused by his alcoholic father, but loves him painfully. Told sometimes by Erin, and sometimes by Liam, this is a delightful, and often moving, account of how perceptions can change and feelings deepen. **RA 12+/IL 12+**

The Ropemaker
Peter Dickinson
Macmillan ISBN: 0 330 39713 3 £6.99

For generations, a spell cast by a powerful wizard has protected the Valley from the Emperor's destructive army. However, when the magic begins to weaken, Tilja and Tahl, along with their respective grandparents, embark on a dangerous journey in an attempt to restore it. Tilja gradually discovers that she has magical powers, which can be used to counterbalance the evil magic they encounter on their quest. This rich fantasy adventure takes the reader on an exciting, magical journey, with many surprises along the way. **RA 12+/IL 12+**

A Step From Heaven
An Na
Allen & Unwin ISBN: 1 86508 793 9 £5.99

Young Ju and her parents move from their home in Korea to start a new and better life in 'Mi Gook' (America). She believes they are travelling to heaven, so is bewildered when they arrive in America where everything is different – the language, food, clothes, even the colour of people's hair. This beautifully written, powerful novel follows Young Ju from the age of four through to her teenage years. It explores her confusion and frustration as she struggles to grow up in two very different cultures and also tackles the issue of domestic violence. **RA 12+/IL 12+**

Corbenic
Catherine Fisher
Red Fox ISBN: 0 09 943848 8 £4.99

Teenager Cal, desperately seeks escape from his dependent, alcoholic mother. On a train journey to visit his uncle, he falls asleep and, awaking in panic, gets off at the wrong station. In the wet, bleak night his travels begin, taking him into a world of otherness: Corbenic. Cal drifts between reality and unreality, haunted by strong Arthurian images, while the needs of his mother, and his refusal to acknowledge her, battle in his head. Unavoidable challenges force Cal to reassess his twenty-first century values. Echoes of chivalry stalk the pages of this mystical novel about facing-up, forgiving and moving on. The atmosphere excites and chills, and the language is compelling. **RA 12+/IL 12+**

Deucalion
Brian Caswell
Floris ISBN: 0 86315 375 5 £4.99
As Old Earth runs out of natural resources, its inhabitants travel across time and space to start a new life on the planet Deucalion. They are promised freedom and a better quality of life, but the reality is very different: they are governed by a tyrant who will wipe out anyone who stands between him and total domination; and the indigenous population, the Elokoi, has been decimated, subdued and illegally subjected to genetic experimentation. The novel recounts, from diverse viewpoints, the attempts to restore both their heritage and genuine democracy. A fascinating book, with a wealth of possibilities for philosophical and ethical discussion. **RA 12+/IL 12+**

Stargirl
Jerry Spinelli
Orchard Books ISBN: 1 84121 926 6 £4.99
Stargirl Caraway arrives at her new school with a unique dress sense and a ukulele. After some debate, the bemused students decide that she is actually quite cool and for a while she even becomes something of an idol. However, the book deftly depicts the fickle side of human nature and its suspicion of anything which refuses to conform. Despite her contemporaries turning against her, Stargirl's innocent appeal and consideration for others never falters. Meanwhile, narrator Leo struggles with his deep affection for the captivating Stargirl and his need for acceptance from his peers. A memorable read, which leaves the reader with a lasting sense of having been touched by someone very special. **RA 12+/IL 12+**

Girl in the Attic
Valerie Mendes
Simon & Schuster ISBN: 0 689 83680 5 £4.99
Nathan's mum decides that moving to Cornwall will help her to put her failed marriage and old life behind her. Nathan, missing his dad and best friend, Tom, is desperate to return to London, until he finds a cottage by the sea and a mysterious girl in the attic – Rosalie. As she struggles to cope with her mother's death and a drunken, bullying father, and Nathan strives to help her, they both learn a lot about love and friendship, and Nathan begins to explore his own feelings about relationships. An exciting, well-paced story, which also raises some pertinent issues for teenagers, especially the difficulties of a family break-up. **RA 11+/IL 12+**

Last Chance
Patrick Cave
Oxford University Press ISBN: 0 19 275241 3 £4.99
Julian returns home from school one day to find that his father has gone, leaving him with sole responsibility for his six-year-old twin sisters. He copes at first, but gradually the pressure of juggling schoolwork, cross-county running, shopping, cleaning and the care of the twins becomes too much. His sisters become increasingly difficult and Julian is sure their bad behaviour is caused by an unhealthy fixation with Fuzzballs, the latest toy craze to sweep the country. Convinced the Fuzzball manufacturers are involved in a sinister scheme, Julian becomes obsessed with uncovering the truth and sets off to investigate. This compelling tale, which highlights the effects of stress, pressures of parenthood and addiction, is a most unusual and rewarding read. **RA 12+/IL 12+**

Revenge House
Bernard Ashley
Orchard Books ISBN: 1 84121 814 6 £4.99
Sophia Micheli loves living in London, but when her father is killed in a horrific hit-and-run accident, everything changes. Her mother has to get away from the city, so they move to a remote house on Romney Marsh to run a B&B. Sophia hates it, until she meets Sol, and the endless peace and quiet gradually become more bearable. Alongside this story runs a contrasting tale of violence and betrayal between ruthless criminals, and when these two worlds collide the Michelis' lives are suddenly in danger. An unusual, but enjoyable, combination of gripping thriller, family drama and teenage love story. **RA 11+/IL 12+**

Raider's Tide
Maggie Prince
Collins ISBN: 0 00 712403 1 £4.99
Beatrice and Verity's lives are mapped out for them. Soon they will marry their cousins and continue the family tradition of farming in the Borderlands of Northern England. But this is the sixteenth century, and when the marauding Scots cross the border to raid and pillage, life is thrown into chaos; an injured Scotsman hiding in the woods changes the course of Beatrice's future. This novel brings home the harsh reality of a life in which surviving from one day to the next is a challenge in itself. An absorbing historical adventure/romance, full of fascinating detail and feisty characters. **RA 12+/IL 12+**

Mondays are Red
Nicola Morgan
Hodder Children's Books ISBN: 0 340 85556 8 £5.99
When Luke Patterson wakes up in hospital after almost dying of meningitis, his family are overwhelmingly relieved. Luke, on the other hand, is confused. Something has happened to his brain – it is full of strange sensations and colours and is inhabited by an evil, megalomaniac morph named Dreeg. As Luke struggles to regain his physical fitness, his mind plays bizarre and dangerous tricks on him – but not all the danger is in his mind. This startlingly original novel explores the power of language and uses words in a remarkable way. A challenging read for young adults. **RA 11+/IL 13+**

Thursday's Child
Sonya Hartnett
Walker Books ISBN: 0 7445 5996 0 £4.99
During the Australian inter-war depression, Harper Flute watches as her family struggles to survive on the barren, arid land. When Caffy is born, Harper's younger brother, Tin, retreats under the shanty to dig a series of tunnels – with calamitous results. Tin continues to dig, 'because that's what he does', and becomes even more reclusive, until he discovers what is going on above and makes a shocking and dramatic appearance. A brilliant, poignant and thought-provoking novel, which will linger long in the reader's mind. **RA 12+/IL 13+**

Massive
Julia Bell
Young Picador ISBN: 0 330 41547 6 £9.99
Fourteen-year-old Carmen has never had a normal relationship with food, due to her mother's obsession with being thin. When they suddenly move to Birmingham, Carmen loses her stepfather, her friends and her home. She enters an unhappy, confused world, where friendship is dependent on looks, and love is expressed by too much or too little food. It is only when her mother is hospitalised and Carmen goes to live with her aunt that life can take on the kind of normality and stability that she needs. A powerful, at times disturbing and unflinching, portrayal of eating disorders and the need for nourishment – in all its forms. **RA 12+/IL 13+**

Between You and Me
Julia Clarke
Oxford University Press ISBN: 0 19 275234 0 £4.99
Jade, a privileged and popular 16-year-old, has to do some
serious growing up when she falls out with the 'new girl' at
school, finds out that her best friend, Jack, is gay, and discovers
that her doting parents have been keeping a huge secret from
her. With humour provided by a delinquent dog, and romance by
a tall, dark stranger, this book makes for compelling reading.
Suspenseful, angst-ridden and extremely well written, this is a
realistic 'teenager growing up' story. **RA 12+/IL 13+**

Remembrance
Theresa Breslin
Corgi ISBN: 0 552 54738 7 £5.99
Events of the First World War are seen through the eyes of a
group of teenagers from two Scottish families with very different
social backgrounds. Charlotte and Maggie want to do something
worthwhile, so they train to be nurses and are sent to France.
Francis, Charlotte's older brother, struggles with his conscience
about the senselessness of the combat, while Maggie's
brothers, John Malcolm and Alex, are seduced by the glory of
war and cannot wait to join up. Despite their social differences,
the horrors of trench warfare and the devastating reality of the
war engulf them all. Breslin's beautiful prose gives the
harrowing sights and sounds of war a human edge.
RA 12+/IL 13+

Warehouse
Keith Gray
Red Fox ISBN: 0 09 941425 2 £4.99
Three seemingly disparate stories are interwoven in this novel
for older readers. Robbie is taken to the warehouse for respite,
after his brother has beaten him up again; Amy is half-playing at
running away from home, after she has been robbed; and Lem,
considered the master of the warehouse, has set its single rule
– no drugs. All their stories are linked by Canner (the real
master of the warehouse), the boy who can and will steal
anything, and by Riley – a thief of a different sort. What begins
by looking simple becomes richly complex. The moral issues
raised are immensely worthwhile, the structure is ingenious, and
the novel is likely to go on resonating in the minds of its readers
for a long time. **RA 12+/IL 13+**

Best BOOK
GUIDE

Young Adult Readers 14+

This section features books which many might class as adult fiction. They present extremely challenging reads, often tackling sensitive and emotionally demanding subjects. This section has been expanded this year to reflect the increasing amount of excellent fiction currently being published for this age group.

Photograph by Susan Gordon-Brown, taken from *Jinx* by Margaret Wild, reproduced by permission of Allen & Unwin

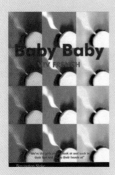

Baby Baby
Viv French
Barrington Stoke ISBN: 1 84299 061 6 £4.50
An easy to read, direct style makes this novel, about two very different girls who become pregnant at the age of fifteen, accessible to a wide range of readers. The author pulls no punches in her description of the hostility Pinkie and April experience from family, friends and strangers, nor does she hide the difficulties they face: at the end of the book we still don't know the fate of Pinkie's gravely ill baby. A book to make readers think hard about the consequences of impulsive actions, relationships, and moral judgements. **RA 9+/IL 13+**

Twocking
Eric Brown
Barrington Stoke ISBN: 1 84299 042 X £4.50
Fifteen-year-old Joey is crazy about Emma, but she likes excitement, particularly TWOCKING (taking cars without the owner's consent), and if Joey wants to be with her, he has to join in. At first, he finds speeding along the motorway in a stolen car thrilling, and is delighted with the money they get for collecting drugs for eighteen-year-old Skelly. However, the inevitable tragedy – a double tragedy, as things turn out – is not far away, and Joey is left with nothing but bitter regrets. This powerful story is written with the pace and straightforward language that would appeal to reluctant teenage readers.
RA 9+/IL 13+

Exodus
Julie Bertagna
Young Picador ISBN: 0 330 40096 7 £9.99
At the turn of the next century, global warming has reached extremes. The polar ice caps have melted and the world is drowning. As Mara's island is swallowed up by the advancing ocean, she becomes one of thousands of refugees seeking sanctuary in the 'cities in the sky' of the New World. The city administrators, however, are elitist, cruel and discriminatory – excluding all outsiders except those they kidnap to use as slave labour. Such a regime can only be changed from the inside, and, despite the dangers, this is exactly what Mara sets out to do. A disturbing and relevant epic, exploring many contemporary themes. **RA 12+/IL 13+**

Merlin, Movies and Lucy Something
John Farman
Piccadilly Press ISBN: 1 85340 755 0 £5.99
This humorous and up-beat diary follows Joe Derby and his
best mate, Merlin, as they experience the highs and lows of life
at 16. Both have girl trouble in different guises, together they
make a serious horror movie which turns out to be the comedy
hit of the year, and Joe has to cope with the death of someone
very close to him. This book is funny, touching, convincing and
highly addictive – it also deals with a number of serious issues.
Refreshing to see teenage issues explored from a boy's point of
view. **RA 11+/IL 14+**

Disconnected
Sherry Ashworth
CollinsFlamingo ISBN: 0 00 712045 1 £4.99
Catherine Holmes is an excellent student about to take her A-
levels. Her teachers and her wealthy parents have high
expectations of her, and under the mounting pressure, Catherine
snaps. She stops working towards her exams and starts drinking
heavily. She falls for Taz, an Asian art student, and starts
hanging around with his down-and-out friends in the park.
Catherine's life whirls downwards when she meets Jan, a
streetwise girl with a dark secret. Discovering the truth about
both Taz and Jan leads Catherine to a painful disillusionment.
This novel deals sensitively with difficult issues and the
characters are portrayed with much skill. **RA 12+/IL 14+**

The House of the Scorpion
Nancy Farmer
Simon & Schuster ISBN: 0 689 83687 2 £7.99
Matt Alacrán is a clone of El Patrón, an evil, megalomaniac
drugs baron who has created his own dystopia in the strip of
land between the United States and Aztlan (formerly known as
Mexico). With his enormous wealth, and the help of unethical
doctors, El Patrón has managed to defy nature and is now
approaching 150-years-old. Although Matt is vilified by all
around him, El Patrón seems to love him and makes sure he
has everything he could want. Matt dreams of one day inheriting
the empire of Opium, but when he eventually becomes aware of
the horrible fate El Patrón really has in store for him, he must
escape or die. A courageous and gripping science fiction
adventure. **RA 12+/IL 13+**

Jinx
Margaret Wild
Allen & Unwin ISBN: 1 86508 264 3 £5.99
Grace, Jen's sister, has Down's Syndrome; her mother is
desperately lonely; her stepmother has cancer; her friend
Connie is gay and afraid to tell her parents, while Serena's
parents shower her with material possessions but barely notice
her. Jen's life seems relatively simple in comparison, until one
boyfriend commits suicide and the next dies in a freak accident,
so she becomes convinced that she is somehow to blame.
Written as a series of sensational short poems, exploring the
nature and effects of love, loss, grief, courage and joy, this book
will make you laugh out loud and bring you close to tears. Truly
memorable. **RA 12+/IL 14+**

Playing With Fire
Henning Mankell, translated by Anna Paterson
Allen & Unwin ISBN: 1 86508 714 9 £5.99
When Sofia's beautiful sister Rosa falls ill and is eventually
diagnosed with AIDS, there are no drugs, no hospital treatment
and no counselling to help the family in rural Mozambique. Sofia
has her own problems – having lost her legs in a landmine
explosion – but at least her disability won't kill her. Sofia and her
mother struggle to support the family and, in their different
ways, to help Rosa face up to her illness and its inevitable
consequences. This brave, moving and honest story paints an
intimate portrait of life on the edge. **RA 11+/IL 14+**

The Facts Speak for Themselves
Brock Cole
Young Picador ISBN: 0 330 41549 2 £8.99
When, aged 13, Linda becomes mixed up in the murder of one
man and the suicide of another, a social worker has to write a
preliminary report on her. But Linda is not happy with it and
insists on writing her own version of the truth. She tells a tale of
abuse, abandonment, neglect and pain, without a hint of
sentiment or self-pity. Her story will arouse indignation, anger
and outrage in the reader, but its overwhelming legacy is one of
terrible sadness and an uneasy sense that the facts do not
always speak for themselves. Contains disturbing material, only
suitable for older readers. **RA 11+/IL 14+**

Poetry

See You Later, Escalator (Oxford University Press) is an anthology of rhymes and poems chosen by John Foster for the very young. A focus on rhythmical and rhyming verse means this book is well stocked with poems that are ideal for reading aloud, learning by heart or staged performance. Tigers, wasps, scarecrows and Billy the Bubble Gum Blower all dance their way through the pages and a variety of illustrators, including Tony Ross, contribute to this appealing publication.

Pip (Scholastic) is a wonderful collection of poetry for young children, written by Tony Mitton and illustrated by Peter Bailey. There is something for everyone here, from humour and fantasy to adventure and animal poems, as well as a story in verse, 'The Woodcutter's Daughter'. Ideal for children aged 6 and over.

Allan Ahlberg's *Friendly Matches* (Puffin) is an entertaining, and at times thought-provoking, collection of poetry about football. From 'The Song of the Referee' to memories of the 1966 World Cup, many aspects of the game are explored using different styles of verse. Complemented by black and white line drawings by Fritz Wegner, this book is sure to appeal to a wide audience, particularly boys.

Former Children's Laureate, Anne Fine, has selected some marvellous poems, both classic and contemporary, for inclusion in her trio of poetry anthologies, *A Shame to Miss 1, 2* and *3* (Corgi). She has added brief comments about what the poems mean to her and how we might understand them better. Volumes 1 and 2 are aimed at junior readers, while volume 3 would appeal to teenagers.

No teenager can claim poetry is irrelevant, boring and difficult after dipping into *Poems with Attitude (Uncensored)* by Andrew Fusek Peters and Polly Peters (Hodder Wayland). The poems are aimed at teenagers, written with a teenage voice and their subjects are those which preoccupy the early to mid-teens especially. There are over sixty poems, varying from ballads to free verse, divided into sections – relationships, school, sex, family, drinks and drugs and so forth. The final section, 'Notes to the Reader', includes explanations about the forms of verse used, some personal notes giving the background or inspiration for a poem and some biographical detail.

In this unusual and moving collection, *Carrying the Elephant: A Memoir of Love and Loss* (Penguin), Michael Rosen tells the story of his life in short episodes, each beautifully written and gives the reader a glimpse into his experiences. Sometimes the incidents are narrated quite directly and at other times simply suggested making this a moving and unforgettable memoir for young adults.

Non-fiction

The Bodley Head publishes an exciting range of pop-up non-fiction books for children aged 7 and over. With flaps to lift, tabs to pull, wheels to turn and a variety of pop-ups, these books are fun, interactive and informative resources. Titles include: *The Great Grammar Book*, *The Terrific Times Tables Book*, *The Magnificent Music Book* and *The Super Science Book*.

The **Art Revolutions** series (Chrysalis) examines the major art movements of the twentieth century. Difficult concepts are explained clearly with concise text and there are activities to

encourage children to experiment with their own art. Each book is illustrated with examples of some major works of art. Suitable for children aged 8 and over. Titles include: *Cubism*, *Impressionism*, *Pop Art* and *Surrealism*.

Franklin Watts' **Artists in Their World** series highlights some of the most influential artists of our time, exploring their work in relation to their lives and world events of the time. Suitable for children aged 9 and over. Titles include: *Salvador Dali*, *Paul Gauguin*, *Vincent van Gogh*, *Frida Kahlo*, *Paul Klee*, *Henri Matisse*, *Claude Monet*, *Pablo Picasso* and *Andy Warhol*.

Each book in the **Introducing Composers** series (Belitha Press) concentrates on a world famous composer, giving young readers an insight into their life and work. Ideal for key stages 2 and 3. Titles include: *Bach*, *Beethoven*, *Chopin*, *Mozart*, *Stravinsky*, *Verdi* and *Vivaldi*.

Books in the **I Can Remember** series (Franklin Watts) series are full of interesting accounts from people who have lived in various periods of history. Illustrated with plenty of photographs and images, they bring history to life through personal experiences. Suitable for key stages 2 and 3. Titles include: *I Can Remember World War II*, *1950s*, *1960s* and *1970s*.

Books in the **My Story** series (Scholastic) are fictional accounts of real historical events, written in diary form. Each title is supported by background notes, a timeline, maps and photographs and are ideal for key stage 3. Titles include: *Mayflower*, *Agincourt*, *Suffragette*, *Waterloo*, *Slave Girl* and *Voyage on the Great Titanic*.

Titles in the **Usborne Better English** series are large-format colourful guides full of clear explanations and practical activities. These titles have been designed to help children aged 8 and over understand the way language is structured and functions and are essential resources to use in the classroom and out of school. Titles include: *Grammar*, *Spelling*, *Punctuation* and *Improve Your English*.

Usborne Language Guides are designed to introduce children to a variety of languages (German, Italian, Spanish, French, Welsh and Irish). Each book includes puzzles, quizzes, word searches and matching games to reinforce grammar and vocabulary and is accompanied by either a CD or a cassette. Suitable for children aged 9 and over.

Title index

Title index

Author/Illustrator index

Best BOOK GUIDE

Author/Illustrator index

Subject index

Subject index

Subject index

Subject index

Subject index

Subject index

BOOKTRUSTED NEWS

Why not subscribe to our colourful quarterly magazine that features news and views on various aspects of the children's book world.

Each issue concentrates on a particular theme and contains a related booklist. Also included are author and illustrator profiles, information about book prizes, reviews of new titles and a variety of articles about children's books and reading. Previous issues include: *Fantasy*; *Disability*; *Refugees*; *Film and TV*; *History* (*World War I and II*); and *Citizenship* (*Bullying*).

Booktrusted News is published four times a year by Booktrust. It is available on annual subscription of £25, which includes a copy of the *Best Book Guide*.

For further information about our publications, subscription service or Children's Book Week materials, please send an A4 SAE to:

The Children's Literature Team
Booktrust
Book House
45 East Hill
London SW18 2QZ

Alternatively, email: Deborah@booktrust.org.uk
telephone: 020 8516 2981
or see our website: **www.booktrusted.com**